Resist Dyeing

www.royalcollins.com

GREAT CHINESE INVENTIONS

Resist Dyeing

Edited by
Hua Jueming and Feng Lisheng

By Zhao Hansheng

Translated by
Chen Wei and Xu Xianwei
(Jiangnan University)

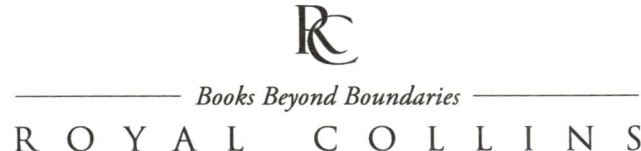

Books Beyond Boundaries

ROYAL COLLINS

Great Chinese Inventions:
Resist Dyeing

Edited by Hua Jueming and Feng Lisheng
By Zhao Hansheng
Translated by Chen Wei and Xu Xianwei (Jiangnan University)

Project Coordinator: Zhang Shaowen and Wang Xiaoyuan

First published in 2025 by Royal Collins Publishing Group Inc.
Groupe Publication Royal Collins Inc.
550-555 boul. René-Lévesque O Montréal (Québec) H2Z1B1 Canada

10 9 8 7 6 5 4 3 2 1

ISBN: 978-1-4878-1283-6

To find out more about our publications,
please visit www.royalcollins.com.

Contents

Preface

The "Four Great Inventions" of China have attracted significant attention from the Chinese people due to their profound impact on the course of modern world history. The term "Four Great Inventions" is widely known, but it originated from Western scholars. While this term holds classical significance, it carries a specific background and meaning. However, it fails to comprehensively reflect the significant inventions and technological cultural traditions of China. Throughout its five-thousand-year history of civilization, China's major inventions far exceed these four great inventions. Since the 20th century, especially in recent decades, China's science and technology have undergone rapid development, playing an increasingly important role in social and economic development. The question of what great inventions and creations exist in Chinese history has become a matter of concern not only for the academic community but also for the public. To answer this question truthfully, objectively, and scientifically, further exploration and sorting are needed based on the study of the history of science and technology in China. This involves selecting major inventions that are original, distinct in character, and have made outstanding contributions and significant impacts on both Chinese and world civilizations and discussing their background and evolutionary processes. To this end, we invited experts in the history of science and related fields to compile the book *Thirty Great Inventions of China*, which was published in May 2017. The book received praise from academia and readers, gaining widespread attention. It was awarded the 13th Wenjin Book Award and the National Excellent Popular Science Works Award by the Ministry of Science and Technology in 2018. It was also selected as one of the "Good Books of China" for 2017 and one of the "40 Most Influential Popular Science Books in China in 40 Years of Reform and Opening Up."

To further promote the research on the history of inventions in China and disseminate knowledge of Chinese science and technology culture, we have organized and compiled the Great Chinese Inventions series based on the book *Thirty Great Inventions of China*. The aim is to provide a more comprehensive and detailed exposition of the significance of major technological inventions in China, to understand their origins and developments, and to enable readers to better comprehend and appreciate the historical and modern value of important ancient Chinese technological inventions and creations. Each book in this series is relatively concise, focusing on knowledge dissemination with rich illustrations, aiming to allow readers to obtain relevant information and knowledge about each invention from the narratives of historians of science and technology in a relatively short period of time.

China boasts a profound history and culture, with the Chinese nation having made numerous great inventions and creations that not only propelled the advancement of Chinese civilization but also exerted significant influence on the progress of world civilization. Every Chinese individual should strive to understand history as accurately as possible. Chinese affairs should be clarified by the Chinese themselves, and Chinese people should have a say in matters of invention and creation. This series of books aims to embody the concept of cultural consciousness and comprehensively summarize the significant contributions of the Chinese nation to human technological civilization as much as possible. In the selection of great inventions, adjustments and expansions have been made, expanding the original thirty inventions to more than forty items, particularly adding significant inventions of modern and contemporary China. This series of books examines Chinese great inventions from both cultural tradition and a global perspective. For instance, Chinese characters and traditional Chinese cooking techniques were previously less regarded as major inventions. Still, they serve as important symbols of Chinese civilization and hold significant positions in Chinese cultural and technological traditions, qualifying as great Chinese inventions. Particularly, Chinese characters, as tools for recording information and expressing thoughts for Chinese people, remain vibrant to this day. They not only play an irreplaceable role in the formation, dissemination, and inheritance of Chinese culture but also have had a significant influence on neighboring countries and regions such as Japan, Korea, and Vietnam. Traditional Chinese cooking techniques have played a crucial role in improving the quality of people's lives and enhancing physical health. With the strengthening of China's comprehensive national strength and international influence, Chinese cooking techniques have spread to various parts of the world and are playing an increasingly important role. Traditional Chinese medicine also embodies some pioneering achievements in modern science and technology, such as the practice of variolation, which is a pioneering immunological achievement with global impact.

We also pay attention to significant inventions in modern and contemporary China. For example, Tu Youyou, representing a group of Chinese scientists, extracted artemisinin, a highly effective and low-toxicity antimalarial drug, based on the inheritance of traditional clinical experience in Chinese medicine and the application of modern scientific methods. After its clinical application, artemisinin has saved the lives of thousands of patients, making a tremendous contribution to human health. Rice is one of the world's major food crops, serving as the staple food for about half the global population. The super hybrid rice cultivation technology invented by Yuan Longping is considered a world-class original and significant invention. Hanzi laser typesetting technology, founded by Wang Xuan, is a great invention in the history of modern printing technology in China. It has played an important role in promoting the dissemination of science and culture. Cultural consciousness is a challenging process. On one hand, we need to understand our technological and cultural traditions to enhance cultural identity and confidence. On the other hand, we need to update and transform our cultural traditions and technology, integrating traditional techniques with modern and foreign technologies and enabling modern technology to take root and develop vigorously in China.

Invention and discovery are inherent drivers of the development of human social civilization. Ancient Chinese science and technology have achieved remarkable success, with our ancestors making significant contributions to the progress of world civilization. Over the past century, China has undergone drastic social changes and cultural transformations, so it is understandable that there haven't been many great inventions and creations during this time. While cherishing and valuing our national cultural traditions and historical experiences, we should also take the initiative in cultural transformation and technological development, continuously enhancing our capacity for independent innovation and making greater contributions to the development of human technology and civilization. Looking at the long-term trend of historical development, Chinese science and technology have entered a new period of accelerated development. The innovation consciousness and capability of the Chinese people have been activated, and we can expect more and more original inventions and creations in the future. The prosperity of Chinese science and technology is something to look forward to.

The question of how many great inventions there have been in Chinese history is subjective, and opinions or disputes are inevitable. We hope that the publication of this series of books will attract more attention and participation from experts and readers, stimulating further discussion and exchanges and contributing to the improvement of related research. We also welcome corrections and feedback from colleagues in the academic community and readers on our work.

Hua Jueming and Feng Lisheng
July 28, 2021

What Is "Resist Dyeing"?

Resist dyeing, similar to tie dyeing, represents several traditional Chinese methods in textile printing and dyeing. This technique, simpler and less technically demanding compared to the complex weaving of brocade and satin, is notable for its straightforward process and easier defect identification, thereby considerably lowering costs. Quickly gaining momentum upon its introduction, resist dyeing thrived for an extended period. It started to decline after the Southern Song Dynasty (1127–1279), surviving predominantly in remote mountain regions and ethnic minority communities. In recent years, with China's increased efforts to promote the protection of traditional crafts and cultural heritage and the implementation of projects to rescue and protect traditional craftsmanship, there has been a rational shift in public consumption attitudes. More and more people are rediscovering their deep interest in these naturally healthy, simple, and elegantly understated traditional handicrafts. Resist dyeing apparel, renowned for its magically varied patterns, vivid colors, and free and easy style, has once again become a fashion trendsetter, turning heads both on the catwalks and in the streets.

The term "resist dyeing" is coined from "resist" and "dyeing," highlighting the two primary techniques used in this craft. "Resist" here means to block dye from penetrating certain areas of the fabric, thus creating patterns. While in a broader sense, textile printing includes methods like resist dyeing, in a narrower context, there is a clear distinction between "printing" and "resist." The Chinese character "印" (print) in oracle bone script consists of a hand claw on the left and a kneeling figure on the right, which together symbolize the act of pressing down. Over time, its meaning evolved: as a noun, it came to refer to stamps or seals, and as a verb, to the act of leaving an imprint by pressing a dye-coated object onto a surface. The character "缬" (resist) initially denoted leaving marks through tying or knotting. This term evolved to encompass a broader range of techniques, including binding, applying lime paste, or using clamps, all integral to the dyeing process. "Dyeing," represented by the character "染," is an ideogram constructed from elements signifying "水" (water), "九" (nine), and "木" (wood). The "water" element symbolizes the solvent essential for dissolving and diluting dyes, which is crucial for achieving uniform color application on fabric. "Wood" represents the origin of these colors, indicating the various plants and trees used as dye sources. Lastly, "nine" metaphorically refers to the frequency of dyeing—not literally nine times, but rather indicating the necessity of multiple applications to attain the desired intensity and variation in color.

The ensuing exposition is structured into two main parts, centering on the pivotal crafts of "resist" and "dyeing" within the production process of resist dyeing. This approach is designed to meticulously showcase and elucidate the developmental trajectory and the significant historical achievements in the technology of resist dyeing.

CHAPTER I

Dyeing the Green Forest into a Brocade Grove— The Art of Brocade Making

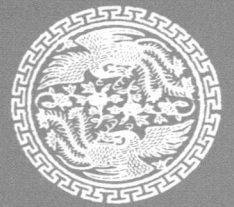

Resist dyeing products, renowned for their exquisite patterns, are often compared to the luxurious and elegant silk brocade and satin and are collectively known as "brocade-patterned resist dyeing" or "resist-dyed brocade." Classified by their crafting techniques, there are three primary forms of resist dyeing: *jiao-xie* (tie resist dyeing), wax resist dyeing, and clamp resist dyeing, collectively known as the ancient "Three Resist Dyeing Techniques." The essence of these techniques lies in resist dyeing, a method that involves applying certain techniques to prevent dye from penetrating the patterned areas of the fabric. For instance, tie resist involves stitch binding, wax resist uses wax, and clamp resist employs stencil plates. Building upon these three methods, the blue calico, also developed from resist dyeing principles, is thus included in the ancient term "Four Resist Dyeing Techniques." A common characteristic of patterns created using resist dyeing techniques is that the final products often exhibit some degree of color spread or crack effect, creating a mesmerizing and magical visual impression. This led to the ancient saying—"In the eyes of the intoxicated, the beauty of resist dyeing emerges."

1. Jiao-Xie *(Tie Resist Dyeing)*

The term *jiao-xie*, also known as *cuo-xie* or *zha-xie*, refers to one of the earliest forms of tie-dyeing. The character "缬" was likely created during the Wei and Jin dynasties (AD 220–420) specifically for this craft, originally denoting just this technique. For instance, ancient rhyming dictionaries like *The Guang Rhyme Dictionary* and *The Expanded Rhymes* variously define the character as "knot" and "patterned silk." *The Sounds and Meanings of All the Classics*, a literature of the Tang Dynasty, elaborates, "Dye the silk by binding it, then reveal the patterns by unbinding the threads; this process is known as tie-dyeing." Similarly, the literature *Rhymes of Ancient and Modern Times* of the Yuan Dynasty states, "Xie denotes the act of tying; it refers to the process of binding silk, then dyeing it to form patterns." It was probably after the Southern and Northern Dynasties (AD 420–589) that the term became a general term for *jiao-xie* crafts. This technique entails meticulously sewing, twisting, and tying the fabric prior to dyeing. This targeted preparation prevents the dye from coloring certain sections of the textile or allows it to seep in varying intensities, thus forming the intended patterns. The charm of *jiao-xie* lies in the subtlety of its hues and the natural gradation at the edges of its patterns, where the dye gently fades from deep to light. This effect lends the fabric a rich, layered appearance, imbued with an artful blend of blurred and shifting patterns, evoking a sense of enchantment. Such a nuanced gradient dye effect is a distinctive quality seldom matched by other dyeing techniques.

1.1 The Origin and Evolution of *Jiao-Xie* Craftsmanship

For a considerable time, scholars believed that *jiao-xie* originated in the Han Dynasty (202 BC–AD 220). This view was dramatically revised in 1995 with the discovery of several *jiao-xie* artifacts in Xinjiang, dating from the 8th to the late 3rd centuries BC. These artifacts, being the oldest known examples of *jiao-xie* in the world, significantly predate the previously assumed timeline. They not only confirm the indigenous origin of *jiao-xie* in China, rather than as a foreign import, but also demonstrate that the craft had already started to develop during the Spring and Autumn and Warring States periods (770–221 BC) by the latest.

During the Wei, Jin, and Southern and Northern Dynasties (AD 220–589), the art of *jiao-xie* reached its zenith. This period's rich production and exquisite craftsmanship are exemplified by the story of Zheng Yun from the Northern Wei Dynasty (AD 386–534), who secured the position of Governor of Anzhou by bribing with approximately 400 *pi* (a traditional unit of cloth measurement) of fine purple *jiao-xie* silk. This substantial amount not only highlights the high value and exquisite quality of these silk pieces but also reflects the large-scale production of *jiao-xie* at the time. However, Zheng Yun's pride was short-lived, as he faced severe rebuke from the respected minister Feng Hui when seeking advice on exploiting Anzhou's wealth, leading to his profound embarrassment.[1] In Volume 9 of *The Latter Records of the Search for Spirits* by Tao Yuanming of the Eastern Jin Dynasty (AD 317–420), there is a notable story, "Before me, two beautiful women appear, as if out of nowhere. They are dressed in a blouse of purple vermillion silk and azure skirt. Remarkably, despite the ongoing rain, their clothes remain dry." The "purple vermillion silk blouse" is believed to reflect the popular fashion of that era, featuring a purple base with white floral patterns reminiscent of deer patterns. Additionally, the term *zuiyan-xie* (intoxicating vermillion silk) first emerged in *Listening to Clothes Pounding at Night*, a poem by Yu Xin, a poet of the Northern Dynasty (AD 386–581), and this term gained widespread popularity later on.

---

1. Li Fang, comp., *Taiping Yulan* (*The Imperial Readings of the Taiping Era*), ed. Sun Yongchang and Xiong Yulan, vol. 7 (Hebei Education Publishing House, 1994), 574.

A wealth of *jiao-xie* artifacts from this era has been excavated, predominantly in northwest China. Notable discoveries include the Former Qin's bright red *jiao-xie* silk from the Astana Cemetery in Turpan, Xinjiang; red and deep red *jiao-xie* silks from the Western Liang period; a red *jiao-xie* silk from the Northern Dynasties found at the ancient city site of Wuyulaik in Yutian County, Xinjiang; a blue *jiao-xie* silk from the Western Liang period unearthed at the Buddha Temple in Dunhuang, Gansu; and fragments of a purple *jiao-xie* blouse from the Former Qin period in the Huahai Bijiatai Cemetery in Gansu. These artifacts, with their clear and detailed patterns, provide a tangible, detailed window into the craft's sophistication and aesthetic inclinations of that era.

During the Sui, Tang, and Five Dynasties (AD 581–960), the development of *jiao-xie* reached its zenith. Exquisite and luxurious *jiao-xie* products had become the premier fashion choice for noblewomen, as well as for courtesans and dancers. *The Book of Sui* records that during the reign of Emperor Wen (AD 581–604), it was considered an honor for court officials and attendants to wear small-flowered vermillion silk garments. During the Tang Dynasty (AD 618–907), various types of dyed *jiao-xie* mentioned in literature included *shu-xie, paihua shu-xie, sui-xie, zuiyan-xie, hong-xie, yuzi-xie, yuzi* deep red *jiao-xie, tan-xie, cuo-xie* (pinched tie-dye), *yuannuo-xie, feng-xie, heluo paikan jiao-xie, tuangong-xie, fan-xie, xi-xie, gaolong-xie, hanyan san-xie* (smoke-veiled *jiao-xie*), among nearly twenty kinds. Most of these names refer to *jiao-xie*, mixed with other dyeing methods. *Shu-xie* and *paihua shu-xie* are believed to represent a unique form of *jiao-xie* textile art originating from the ancient Shu region, now modern-day Sichuan Province. This specific style is referenced in Bai Juyi's poem about "Chengdu's newly crafted *jiao-xie*" and also described in *The Book of Tang* as *shu-xie* robes. *Sui-xie* is a small-flowered *jiao-xie. Zuiyan-xie*, with a pattern resembling blurred drunken eyes, is another form of *jiao-xie. Hong-xie* is *jiao-xie* with either a red base or floral pattern. *Yuzi-xie* and *yuzi* deep red *jiao-xie*, having fish-roe-like patterns, are among the simpler *jiao-xie* varieties to produce. *Tan-xie*, named for its light ochre color, is another specific kind of *jiao-xie. Cuo-xie*, or *cuoyun jiao-xie*, is a more complex variety. *Yuannuo-xie* features mandarin duck patterns on Luo fabric. *Feng-xie* is *jiao-xie* characterized by maple leaf patterns. *Heluo paikan jiao-xie*, with *heluo* meaning a type of loosely woven fabric, and *paikan* suggesting a set design, might be similar to *paihua shu-xie. Tuangong-xie* is a symmetrical floral *jiao-xie*.

In the latter part of the Tang Dynasty, Emperor Wenzong, aiming to suppress the prevailing opulence, issued a decree dictating that women's standard attire should comprise "clothing made of blue-green *jiao-xie* fabric, complemented by simple slippers adorned with small floral patterns."[2] This particular style of blue-green clothing, a common garment for servant women and slaves, gained widespread popularity in remote regions due to its simple craftsmanship. It's recorded that "In the western Yellow River region of Gansu, where silkworms and mulberries are scarce, women donned skirts of blue-green fabric paired with fine cloth."[3] Emperor Wenzong's initiative to promote simplicity over extravagance, substituting the intricately dyed, luxurious *jiao-xie* goods with the modest blue-green variant, had little effect on the well-entrenched fashion sensibilities revered and imitated by women since the Tang Dynasty's zenith. Poet Xu Yin's verses, "Noble ladies treasure their smoke-veiled *jiao-xie*, while fallen coin purses lie unclaimed by lesser courtesans," not only highlight the enchantment of *jiao-xie* but also underscore the aristocratic women's blatant disregard for the imperial edict, as exemplified by their indifference to lost coin purses.

In the extant paintings from the Tang and Five Dynasties periods, the delicate and vividly colored attire worn by women predominantly consists of *jiao-xie* products. A notable example is Zhou Fang's *Court Ladies Adorning Their Hair with Flowers* from the Tang era, preserved in the Liaoning Provincial Museum (Figure 1.1). This artwork portrays five court ladies and a female attendant embellished with a small dog, a white crane, and magnolia flowers. In it, the intricate patterns on the inner long skirts and the outer garments' resist white patterns of the three ladies are distinctly visible, suggesting *jiao-xie*, possibly of the *cuoyun jiao-xie* variety, a technique known for its distinctive blurred or smudged effects. The *Court Ladies Preparing Newly Woven Silk* by Zhang Xuan of the Tang Dynasty, housed in the Museum of Fine Arts Boston (Figure 1.2), depicts a scene of Tang aristocratic women engaging in silk preparation and sewing. The women in this painting are all clad in *jiao-xie* clothing, especially a woman fanning the fire near a stove in a green *jiao-xie* skirt with alternating pink floral motifs on a white background, showcasing remarkable craftsmanship. Gu Hongzhong's *Night Revels of Han Xizai* from the Southern Tang States during the Five Dynasties, preserved in the Palace Museum in Beijing (Figure 1.3), captures an evening banquet at Han Xizai's residence. The three women on the couch in this painting feature large, smoky-patterned circles on their open-front tops, particularly the leftmost woman in a dark blue garment with prominent yellow circles, clearly a product of resist dyeing.

2. Ouyang Xiu and Song Qi, *New Book of Tang*, ed. Chen Huanliang and Wen Hua, vol. 1 (Yuelu Publishing House, 1997), 320.

3. Lü Simian, *History of the Two Jin Dynasties and the Southern and Northern Dynasties*, vol. 2 (Beijing Institute of Technology Press, 2018), 1132.

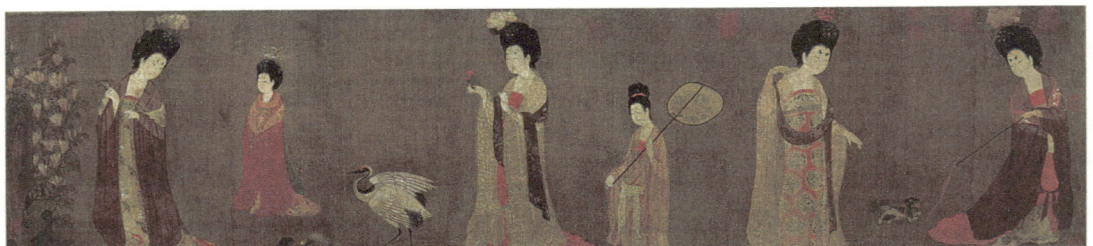

Figure 1.1 *Court Ladies Adorning Their Hair with Flowers*

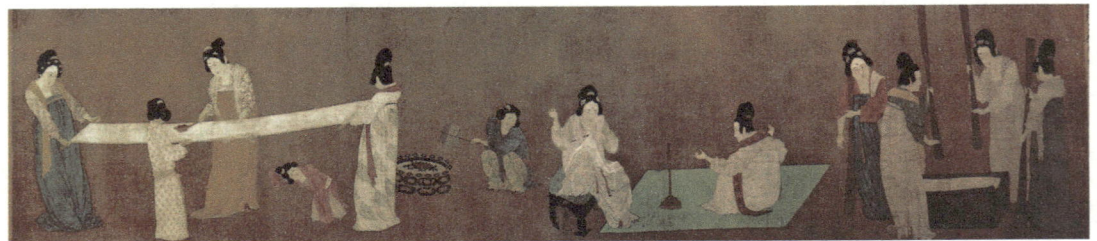

Figure 1.2 *Court Ladies Preparing Newly Woven Silk*

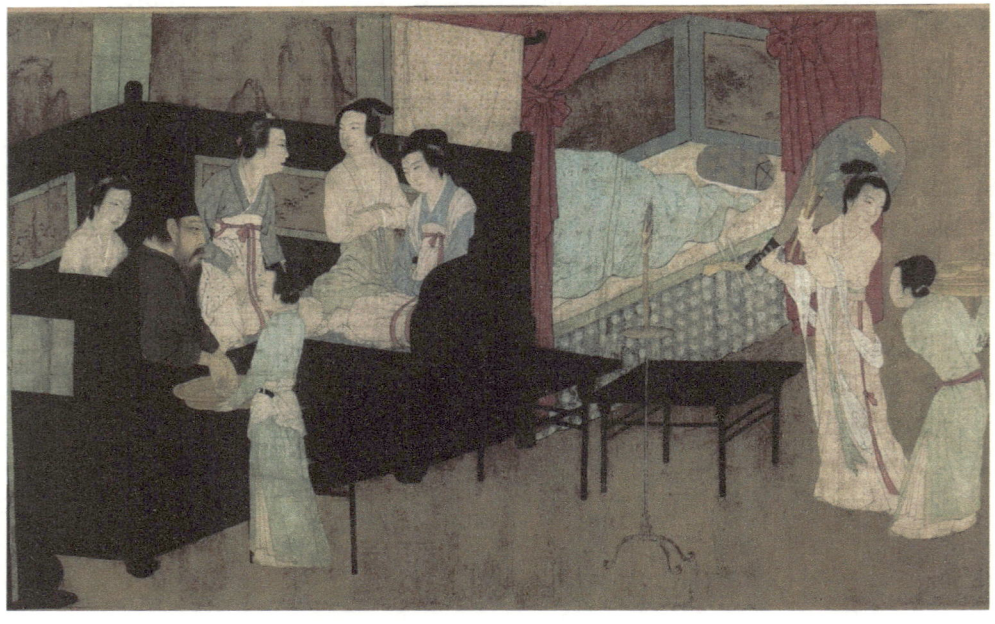

Figure 1.3 *Night Revels of Han Xizai* (partial view)

Tri-colored pottery figurines and pottery from the same era frequently showcase garments and patterns featuring resist dyeing techniques. For instance, the female seated figurine excavated from a Tang Dynasty tomb in Wangjiafen Village, Xi'an, Shaanxi Province (Figure 1.4), dons a blue-green skirt with clusters of small white flowers. This attire represents the standard women's clothing of that time, known as a greenish-blue tie-dyed skirt. Another example is the Tang tri-colored female standing figurine unearthed from the An Yuanshou Tomb in Liquan County, Shaanxi Province (Figure 1.5). This figurine is dressed in a blue robe sparsely decorated with white spots, each centered with a touch of brown, delicately recreating a popular tie-dye pattern from the Tang Dynasty. Additionally, fragments of Tang tri-colored shard found at the Huangye Kiln in Gongyi City, Henan Province (Figure 1.6), display patterns that closely resemble *lutai-xie* (deer-pattern tie-dye), *zuiyan-xie* (drunken-eye tie-dye), or *yuzi-xie* (fish-roe tie-dye). This indicates the Tang people's preference for tie-dye patterns with the gradient dye effect, leading to their creative application on everyday utensils.

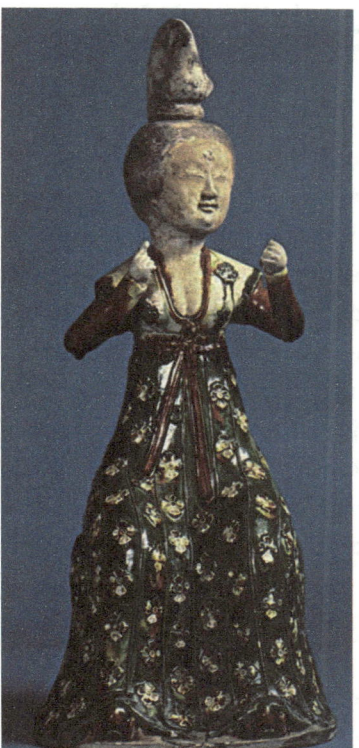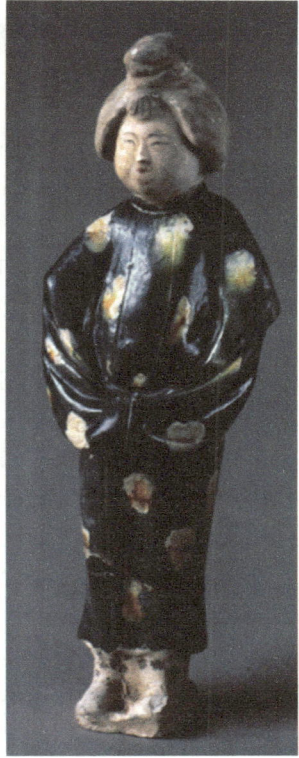

Figure 1.4 (RIGHT) Female seated figurine, Tang Dynasty, excavated in Xi'an, Shaanxi

Figure 1.5 (FAR RIGHT) Tri-colored female standing figurine, Tang Dynasty, excavated in An Yuanshou Tomb, Liquan County, Shaanxi

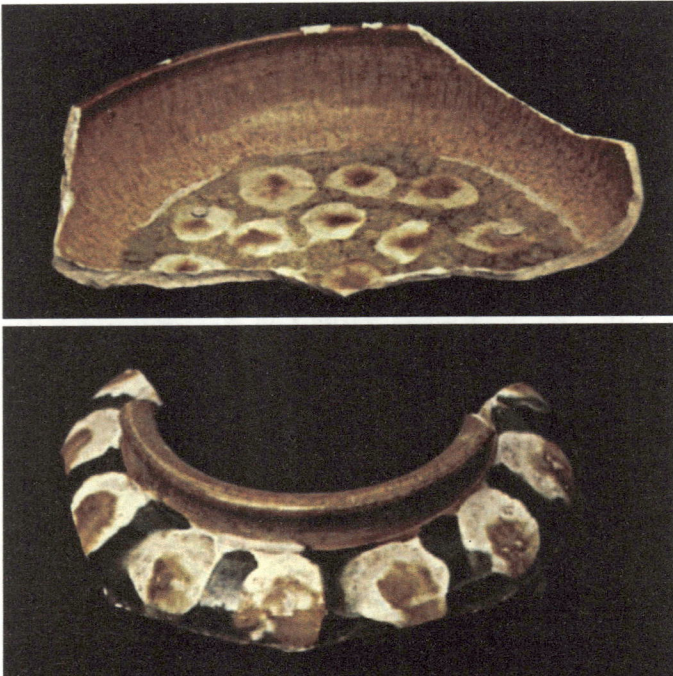

Figure 1.6 Tri-colored Tang Dynasty shard, excavated from Huangye Kiln, Gongyi City, Henan

During the Tang Dynasty, *jiao-xie* was not only popular for women's attire but also extensively utilized in military uniforms. The Tang regulations specified that soldiers' clothing should feature *jiao-xie* as a distinctive identifier. The Imperial Guards, both infantry and cavalry, were required to wear knee-length robes with small sleeves and hats featuring floral *jiao-xie* designs. Notably, three painted pottery figurines of men wearing traditional headgear were excavated from the Tomb of Empress Ai of the Tang Dynasty's Gongling in Yanshi, Henan. These wind hats, similar to the caps featuring floral *jiao-xie* designs worn by Tang soldiers, were commonly matched with knee-length robes and wide-legged pants. Among the *jiao-xie*-related figurines, two showcase black backgrounds with white flowers, and one presents a red background with white flowers. Their garment features a knee-length cape with an attached head covering. While the top of the head covering is adorned with honeysuckle patterns, the rest of the garment is decorated with irregularly arranged, larger circular tie-dye motifs (Figure 1.7).

During the Tang Dynasty, twisted silk products were also used as important trade items for bartering in exchange for production materials. Historical records show that in the third year of Zhenyuan (AD 787), Li Bi suggested, "Now, since the Tubo have been residing in the Yuan and Hui regions, using cattle to transport grain, and when the grain runs out, the cattle become redundant. It is proposed to issue inferior dyed silk from the left treasury, dye it into colorful twisted silk, and then trade it through the Dangxiang (a pastoral tribe living on the Songpan Plateau in Sichuan Province). For each head of cattle, no more than two or three *pi* are needed, amounting to a total of 180,000 *pi*, which can yield more than 60,000 heads of cattle."[4] Tubo was a regime established by ancient Tibetans on the Tibetan Plateau, and the Tangut people were one of the ancient northern ethnic minorities, a branch of the Western Qiang people. This record indicates that the Tang Dynasty lacked plow cattle. Li Bi suggested using low-quality dyed silk textiles to exchange for Tubo's plow cattle through the market, which was clearly a beneficial trade for the Tang Dynasty.

A wealth of artifacts crafted using the traditional Chinese *jiao-xie* silk dyeing technique have been unearthed from this era. Among these discoveries is a remarkable piece of brown silk fabric from the Tang Dynasty, measuring 16 centimeters in length and 5 centimeters in width, found in Tomb No. 117 in the Astana region of Turpan, Xinjiang. This exquisite artifact is distinguished by its gently nuanced color

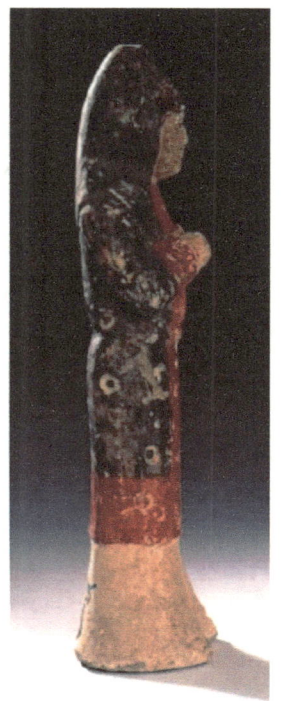

Figure 1.7 Painted male figurine with headgear from the Tomb of Empress Ai of the Tang Dynasty's Gongling, Yanshi, Henan

scheme, with the pattern edges showcasing natural, gradient hues that result from the dye's absorption. This technique gives the fabric a depth and complexity, creating an enchanting visual effect. Equally striking is a Tang Dynasty skirt unearthed from Tomb No. 308 in Astana, adorned with diamond grid patterns in rich shades of dark and eggplant purple. The skirt's preserved folding marks and threading holes offer insights into its intricate creation process. Before dyeing, the fabric was meticulously folded into strips and gathered along diagonal lines with needle and thread, forming a layered, block-like structure. This pre-dyeing preparation resulted in the fabric's unique, intricately folded pattern—a technique that likely mirrors those documented in historical texts.

---

4. Sima Guang, comp., *Zizhi Tongjian* (*Comprehensive Mirror for Aid in Government*), annot. Hu Sanxing and ed. Zizhi Tongjian Punctuation Team, vol. 16 (Zhonghua Book Company, 1956), 7489.

According to historical records, the *jiao-xie* technique made its way to Japan around the Tang Dynasty and quickly gained widespread popularity. Ancient Japanese documents on tie-dyeing directly adopted the Chinese characters "缬" or "绞缬." The tie-dyeing textiles preserved in the Shosoin Repository, a historical treasure repository located in Nara, Japan, exhibit techniques similar to those later seen in styles like kanoko shibori (deer spot shibori), rasen shibori (dew fairy shibori), and kumo (spider) shibori. Even today, Japanese kimonos featuring fish-roe patterns in *jiao-xie* style, combined with indigenous Japanese motifs, remain highly cherished by the Japanese people.

By the Northern Song period (AD 960–1127), *jiao-xie* continued to flourish. Popular styles included *lutai-xie* (deer pattern tie-dye), *jin-xie* (brocade tie-dye), *jianer-xie* (cocoon tie-dye), *shu-xie* (a regional style), *cuo-xie* (pinched tie-dye), *jiangshui-xie* (starch water tie-dye), *tan-xie*, *zhe-xie* (folded-pattern tie-dye, with "zhe" meaning "folded"), and *santao-xie* (triple-overdye tie-dye). Some names originated in the Tang Dynasty, while others were newer. For instance, *lutai-xie* was distinguished by its yellow-brown base with white spots, known for its unique "raised spotted patterns with varied colors." *Jin-xie* was characterized by geometric patterns that are common in the brocade. *Jianer-xie* featured a pattern of scattered cocoon-shaped dots. *Jiangshui-xie* was named for its technique of using starch mixed with dye paste for printing. *Zhe-xie*, possibly a synonym for a type of stitched tie-dye, might also refer to a painted or directly drawn style. *Santao-xie* involved a complex process of dyeing with three layers of color, creating a rich and intricate appearance. These tie-dye products were so exquisite that they began to rival brocades in the Northern Song Dynasty (960–1127). As a result, the ceremonial units of the court started to use these tie-dye items instead of traditional brocades, and even the embroideries and brocades gifted by the court to officials were replaced with tie-dye fabrics. According to the *History of Song*, the attire of officials and soldiers in the Song court's ceremonial units comprised: ten side officers wearing plain hats, purple silk shirts, tie-dye shirts, and silk belts; forty Yihuang officials donning tie-dye hats, multicolored precious flower patterned shirts, and silk belts; two hundred and ten Wuji soldiers in tie-dye hats, crimson shirts with precious flower patterns, and silk belts; two hundred and seventy Yigong soldiers sporting tie-dye hats, green precious flower patterned shirts, and silk belts; eight people per carriage clad in hats, Yinan tie-dye single-layer shirts, and gold and silver painted branch waist belts; twenty-seven carriage officials wearing turban-like headgear, white lion pattern tie-dye single-layer shirts, gold and silver painted Haijie waist belts, with a triple-layered purple inner garment; the standard attire for ceremonies included tie-dye hats, plain hats, flat turbans, Wubian crowns, multicolored precious flower patterned shirts, and silk belts; the five carriage drivers' attire consisted of flat turbans, green silk forehead bands, tie-dye silk phoenix robes, wide-sleeved crimson tie-dye jackets, silk trousers, socks, and hemp shoes; the carriage officials wore yellow tie-dye phoenix robes, yellow silk belts, purple life-thread sashes, and purple silk tied hangings.

The tie-resist dyeing technique, while not overly complex, requires meticulous execution according to the pattern design, often involving the intricate creation of dozens, hundreds, or even thousands of knots in a single piece of fabric. After the dyeing process, these knots must be delicately unraveled, which demands precision to avoid damaging the fabric, leading to significantly high labor costs. With the decline of national power during the Northern Song Dynasty, the government repeatedly issued decrees prohibiting the civilian use of tie-dye items, dampening its widespread popularity. As documented in the *History of Song · Records of Carriages and Costumes*, several edicts were enacted to restrict tie-dyeing: In the seventh year of the Dazhong Xiangfu era (1014), the public wearing of gold-destroyed and cymbal-cover tie-dye items was banned; in the eighth year (1015), the prohibition extended to soap-striped tie-dye clothes. A decree in the third year of the Tiansheng era (1025) forbade residents in the capital from wearing garments with black-brown bases and white flowers, as well as blue, yellow, or purple bases with pinched blur patterns. It mandated their production to cease within ten days. In the second year of the Zhenghe era (1112), it was decreed that tie-dye silk be produced only for military insignia and guard uniforms, completely barring its civilian creation and use.

The imperial restrictions on tie-resist dyeing production were finally lifted in the early Southern Song Dynasty (1127–1279), leading to a brief resurgence in its popularity. However, this revival was short-lived due to the prolonged effect of the bans and shifts in aesthetic preferences. Eventually, by the Ming and Qing dynasties, tie resist dyeing nearly vanished in the central plains, fading into obscurity in minority regions and remote, inaccessible mountain areas.

1.2 The Craft of *Jiao-Xie*

The art of *jiao-xie* encompasses several key steps: pattern designing, knotting, dyeing, unbinding and washing, and final arrangement.

Pattern designing: Patterns are traced onto the cloth, providing a guideline for subsequent stitching and knotting.

Knotting: Stitching is the primary technique for creating the patterns of tie-resist dyeing, complemented by knotting. This process can be broadly classified into four methods.

The primary method is the sewing and binding technique. This involves executing straight stitches along the periphery of the sketched pattern, generally completing each motif with a single thread. Once stitched, the thread is pulled tight, causing the fabric at the seam to bunch up before being secured with a knot. Subsequently, the excess thread is used to wrap around the stitched area repeatedly, tightening it as necessary to ensure a distinct design outline. The standard for knot tightness varies depending on the fabric's weave density, the dyeing technique, the duration of the dyeing process, and the design requirements. For complex or large designs, a segmented approach may be adopted. Different patterns necessitate distinct straight stitching techniques. Typically, a straight stitch tracing along the pattern's external edge is used for designs with pronounced curves. This involves knotting the thread at the start, pulling it tight after stitching, and then gathering and knotting it at the end. Post-dyeing, designs with shorter stitch intervals appear more defined and precise than those with longer intervals. A dense straight stitch is employed for block patterns composed of line elements, stitching along the inside edge of the pattern. For patterns resembling dashed lines, a looping stitch is used, which involves folding the fabric at the pattern line and stitching around the fold. This tying technique is notable for its versatility and adaptability, which makes it ideal for depicting varied graphic and representational motifs. However, this method is labor-intensive and demands high technical skill (Figure 1.8).

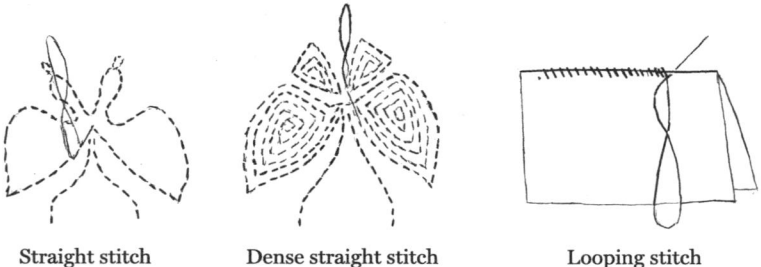

Straight stitch   Dense straight stitch   Looping stitch

Figure 1.8 Diagram of the sewing and binding technique

The second method is the tying and binding technique. This versatile approach doesn't always require a predefined pattern. Simply fold, pinch, or crumple the fabric, then secure it with thread or rope. The bound areas create unique dye-resistant patterns. For example, to achieve continuous stripes, fold or gather the fabric along the warp or the weft, then tie it tightly at intervals with string or rope. For radial square or diamond patterns, fold the fabric repeatedly. Using the central fold as the apex, bind the lower portion with a string or rope. For radial circular patterns, spread the fabric flat. Select a point and pinch it up using your right thumb, index, and middle fingers. Gather the fabric beneath with your left hand and bind it below the pinch point with cotton thread. To create scattered circular motifs, lay the fabric flat. As before, pinch and lift small fabric sections as desired, binding each separately with cotton thread. For continuous patterns, spread the fabric flat and fold it into shapes like squares, diamonds, or triangles. Bind these folded corners with thread or rope. Alternatively, twist the fabric into a rope or braid shape before tying it (Figure 1.9).

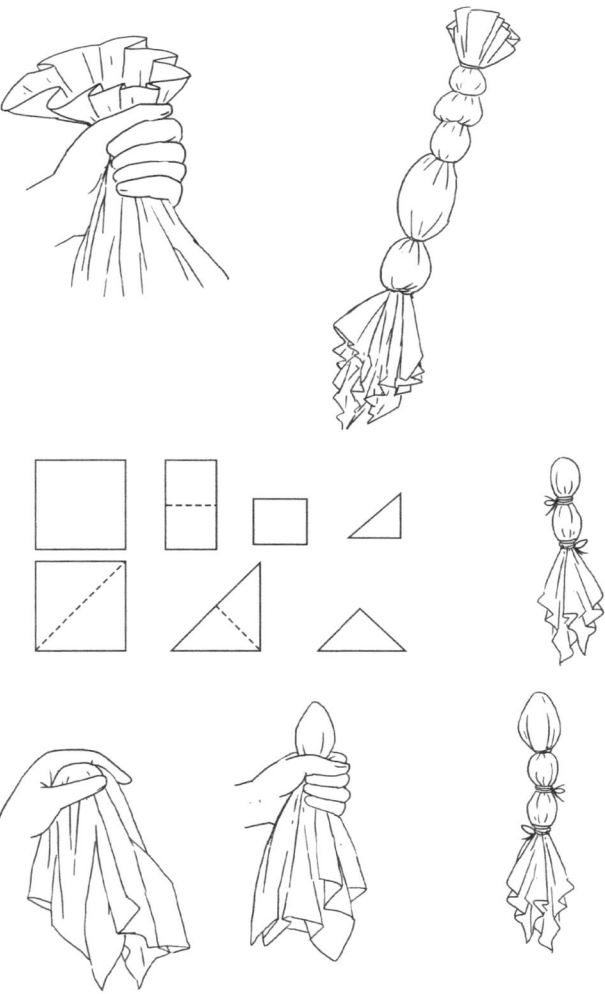

Figure 1.9 Diagram of the tying and binding technique

The third method is the knotting technique. In this approach, the fabric is manipulated and knotted on its own without the use of strings or ropes. These tight knots effectively block the dye during dyeing, creating spontaneous and unstructured patterns. Typically, the fabric is folded in various ways—such as in half, diagonally, or using other methods—before knots are tied in the sections intended for resist dyeing. This technique includes several knot styles, such as the four-corner knot, where the fabric is gathered and knotted at four points, and the triangle knot, involving a three-point gathering and knotting. There is also the fold-over knot, created by folding the fabric upon itself and then tying it (Figure 1.10).

The fourth method is the tool-assisted tying technique. This method involves using a variety of tools to assist in creating intricate patterns, resulting in unique and distinctive designs on the dyed fabric. Objects that retain their shape, such as coins, small stones, or wooden blocks, can be used as padding. These items are encased in the fabric, producing dispersed patterns that mimic their shapes. Additionally, flat tools like bars, squares, or triangles can be employed to clamp the fabric, which is then securely tied with string or rope to create various patterns (Figure 1.11).

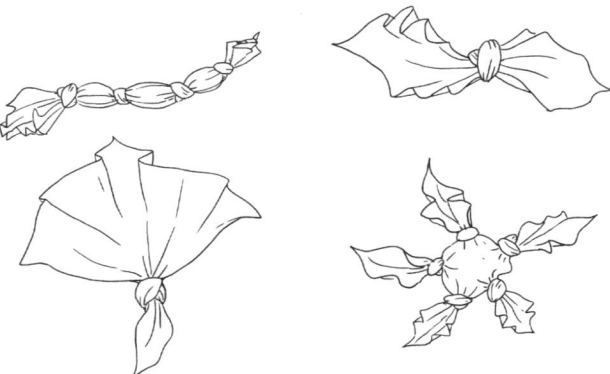

Figure 1.10 Diagram of the knotting technique

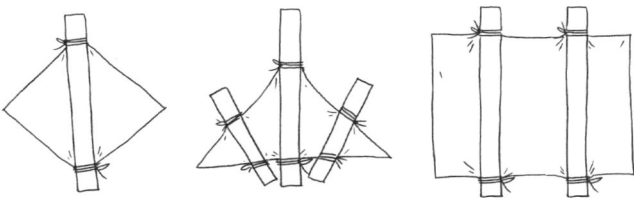

Figure 1.11 Diagram of the tool-assisted tying technique

Dyeing: Begin by soaking the bound fabric thoroughly in clean water, then drain it before immersing it in the dye bath. For single-color dyeing, either use a pre-made dye solution or a custom blend of various dyes for a consistent color achieved in a single session. To create a gradient effect with a single color, from light to dark, first immerse the entire fabric in the dye. After a while, partially lift the fabric out of the dye, gradually increasing the dye concentration for continued dyeing. Repeat this step-by-step process to develop the desired gradient. After the final dyeing, rinse off any excess dye and remove the threads to unveil the subtle gradation effect. In the case of layered color dyeing, it's typical to start with the lightest shade, progress to a medium tone, and conclude with the darkest shade. This method involves precise, manual control over the extent of dyeing in specific areas. Once dyed and unbound, the overlapping colors blend to create new shades, resulting in a fabric with a rich, multi-hued, layered artistic appearance.

Unbinding and washing: After the dyeing process is complete, get the bound materials and rinse them in clean water to wash away any excess dye. Once dry, remove the binding threads or any other auxiliary materials used during the dyeing process. Finally, thoroughly rinse the fabric and let it air dry in a cool, shaded area.

Final arrangement: After unbinding and washing, the fabric will have numerous irregular creases due to the knotting process. It needs to be ironed smooth to fully reveal the visual impact of the tie-dye pattern's colors (Figure 1.12).

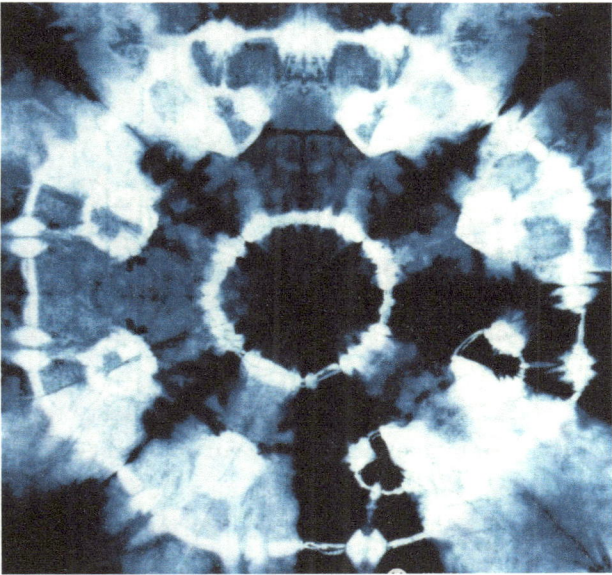

Figure 1.12 Modern tie-dye finished products

1.3 Appreciation of *Jiao-Xie* Artifacts

Ancient *jiao-xie* artifacts, or tie-dye artifacts, with their vibrant colors, intricate designs, and exquisite meanings, appear almost as if naturally formed, inspiring boundless imagination. The majority of these ancient tie-dye artifacts have been found in Xinjiang and Gansu. A large part was discovered by early 20th-century explorers from abroad and is now dispersed among museums in the UK, Germany, Russia, Japan, India, and other countries. The remainder, unearthed after the founding of the People's Republic of China, is primarily housed in cultural institutions in Xinjiang and Gansu, with a few pieces in museums elsewhere. These artifacts showcase various tie-dye techniques, such as stitching, binding, knotting, and clamping, with binding being the most prevalent. The dyeing styles mainly include solid color and layered color dyeing, the latter being more common. Below, we briefly introduce some of the most representative ancient tie-dye pieces.

Figure 1.13 is a tie-dyed woolen checkered plain weave cloth from the Spring and Autumn and Warring States periods, excavated from Tomb No. 1 in Zaghunluq, Qiemo (Cherchen) County, Xinjiang. This piece is preserved in a Xinjiang cultural heritage institution. The artifact features a diamond pattern with naturally occurring gradient effects, indicating that the tie-dye process was meticulously applied to the regular small squares formed by the cross-weaving of the wool. This results in a neatly organized pattern. This artifact stands as one of the earliest examples of tie-dyeing discovered globally.

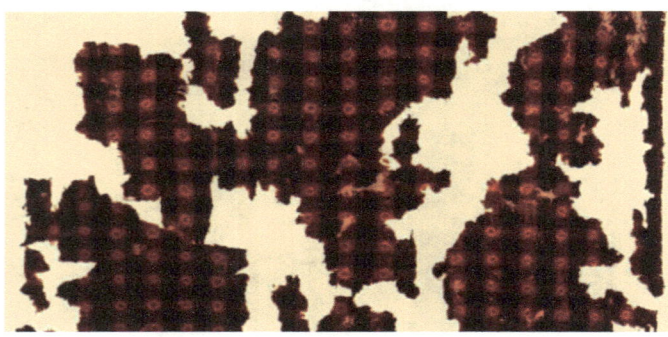

Figure 1.13 A tie-dyed woolen checkered plain weave cloth from the Spring and Autumn and Warring States periods

Figure 1.14 is an ancient woolen garment piece from the Spring and Autumn and Warring States periods and is currently preserved in a Xinjiang cultural heritage institution. This artifact was unearthed from Tomb No. 3 in Zaghunluq, Qiemo (Cherchen) County, Xinjiang, measuring 23 centimeters in length, 9.5 centimeters in width, and 0.12 centimeters in thickness, the garment piece is primarily yellow with red stripes, crafted from wool. Its warp and weft are uniformly dyed yellow, with each thread being about 0.06 to 0.07 centimeters wide, spun in a Z-twist, and woven in a single ply. The garment maintains an average density of 12 threads per centimeter in both directions. The red stripes are the result of a stitch-resist dyeing technique, where folding and stitching create a resist pattern. The process likely involved methodically folding and stitching the yellow wool at set intervals, then dyeing it in red. Post-dyeing, upon unraveling the stitches, the exposed edges reveal red stripes against the yellow base, while the concealed folds retain their original yellow hue, resulting in a distinct pattern. The unevenness in the folding, especially at the fold intersections, contributes to a pronounced wavy appearance on the surface. This piece stands as one of the earliest known examples of tie-dye artifacts in the world.

Figure 1.14 A brown garment with red stripes on a yellow twisted silk background of the Spring and Autumn and Warring States periods

Figure 1.15 displays a bright red tie-dyed silk artifact from the Northern Dynasties period, currently preserved in the Museum of Xinjiang Uygur Autonomous Region. This piece was excavated from Tomb No. 305 in Astana, Turpan. The tie-dye technique used here is the binding method, creating a pattern of scattered dots across the fabric. Each dot is square-shaped, with its diagonals perfectly aligning with the warp and weft of the fabric, a characteristic seen consistently throughout the piece. The center of each square, where the dye has been applied, shows a radial gradient effect, evidently a result of the binding process.

Figure 1.16 is a tie-dyed women's silk garment of the Northern Dynasties period, excavated from Tomb No. 177 in Astana, Turpan, Xinjiang. It is preserved in the China Silk Museum. The garment has a total length of 72 centimeters, with sleeves measuring 192 centimeters in length. It features a

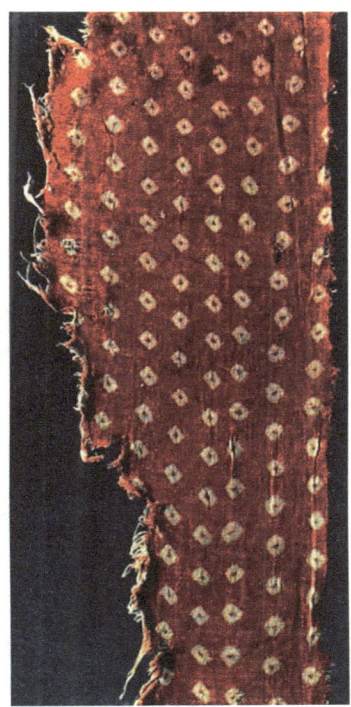

Figure 1.15 A bright red twisted silk brocade of the Northern Dynasties period

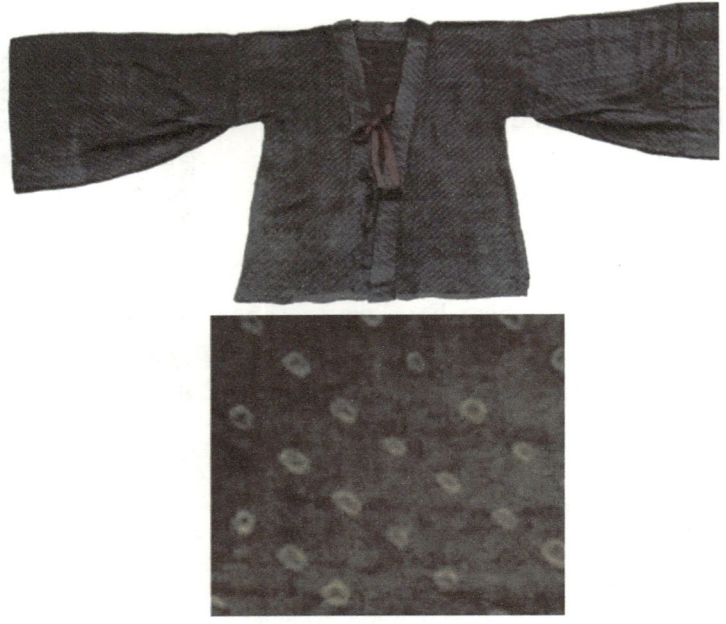

Figure 1.16 A tie-dyed women's silk garment of the Northern Dynasties period

slightly overlapping front with bell-shaped wide sleeves and two red and brown ties at the front. The entire garment is adorned with extremely small tie-dyed patterns, presenting tiny squared dots in a hollow ring shape, arranged in rows that resemble lines from a distance. The fabric used is plain woven silk. These tiny square patterns, each side measuring 0.2 centimeters, were created using the binding method, a traditional "fish roe tie-dye" technique. The vertical spacing between the dots is 1.4 centimeters, and the horizontal spacing is 1 centimeter. The preservation of such a well-preserved Northern Dynasties tie-dyed women's garment among unearthed silk textiles is exceptionally rare.

Figure 1.17 A green tie-dyed silk of the Tang Dynasty

Figure 1.17 is an exquisite piece of green tie-dyed silk from the Tang Dynasty, a treasured exhibit of the

Turpan Museum in Xinjiang. This remarkable silk artifact, which was discovered in Turpan, is notable for its identical patterns on both sides. This symmetry suggests that the tie-dye technique employed was likely the clamping method, a specialized approach within the realm of tool-assisted binding techniques.

Figure 1.18 is a brown tie-dye silk of the Tang Dynasty, also from Astana, Turpan, housed in the Museum of Xinjiang Uygur Autonomous Region. The net-like pattern with varying line thickness and depth in color, along with visible stitching holes, indicates the use of a stitch and knot method. This style was popular in the Tang Dynasty, as reflected in the poet Li He's verse "Drunken tie-dyeing throws a red net," describing the net-patterned tie-dyeing.

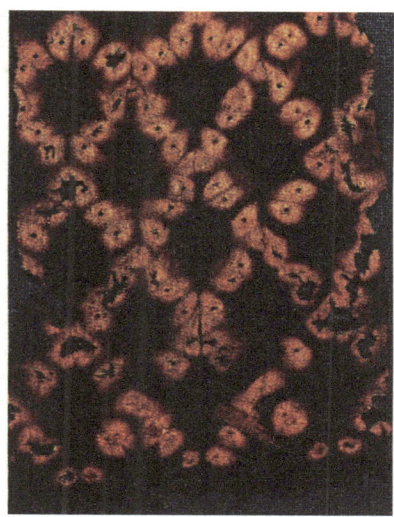

Figure 1.18 A brown tie-dye silk of the Tang Dynasty

Figure 1.19 is a flower-patterned tie-dyed gauze of the Tang Dynasty, a treasured item in the Museum of Xinjiang Uygur Autonomous Region, excavated from the Astana tombs in Turpan.

This is a patterned gauze fabric with a dark green background and four-petaled flower patterns scattered throughout. Each pattern, vaguely square in shape, measures 4 to 5 centimeters on each side, with its diagonals aligning with the warp and weft of the fabric. The tie-dye technique employed here is the stitched resist method. Notably, the presence of light brown halos around the patterns suggests the possibility of two-tone dyeing. This flower tie-dye technique is technically versatile and less restrictive, suitable for both loosely scattered floral designs and more structured decorative patterns. It's particularly effective for dyeing large pieces of fabric.[5] Furthermore,

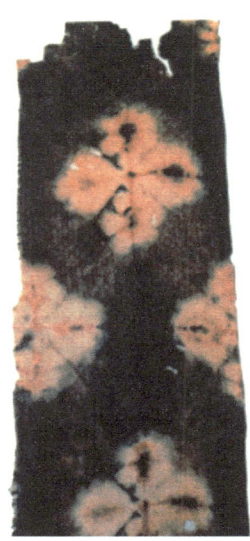

Figure 1.19 A flower-patterned tie-dyed gauze of the Tang Dynasty

the expressive effect of these flowers, resembling blooms shrouded in the morning mist, beautifully echoes the poetic imagery of the Tang Dynasty, reminiscent of lines

5. Wang Xu, *A Collection of Dyeing Techniques* (Yanshan Publishing House, 2014), 74.

Figure 1.20 A tie-dyed gauze of the Southern Song Dynasty

like "light skirts lost in the morning mist amongst flowers and grass," capturing a sense of enchanting ethereality.

Figure 1.20 is a tie-dyed gauze of the Southern Song Dynasty from the Zhou family tomb in De'an, Jiangxi. Although it is difficult to discern the original colors due to long-term water immersion, the arrangement and complexity of the floral patterns are still identifiable. Reportedly, five tie-dyed items were unearthed from the Zhou tomb, including two garments and three fragments, all made using a binding method with a similar pattern arrangement, showing a balance between randomness and meticulous detail. These artifacts from the Zhou tomb are among the rare surviving Southern Song Dynasty tie-dyed items, making them extremely precious.

2. Wax Resist Dyeing

Wax resist dyeing is a traditional technique. The process begins by melting beeswax and then using a four to five-inch bamboo pen or a wax knife made from copper to apply the molten wax onto smooth, flat fabric, creating various designs. Once the wax solidifies, the fabric is dyed in a dye bath and then boiled to remove it. The areas covered in wax resist the dye, remaining uncolored, and thus stand out as white floral patterns against the dyed background. Due to the contraction of the wax as it solidifies and the natural creasing of the fabric, the wax layer often develops numerous cracks. When dyed, the color seeps into these cracks, resulting in unexpected fine, irregular colored lines in the patterns, creating the distinctive decorative effect of batik products.

2.1 The Origin and Evolution of Wax Resist Dyeing

There are different theories in the academic community regarding the time and place of the origin of the wax resist dyeing technique.

One theory is the Egyptian hypothesis. Some scholars believe that as early as 1500 BC, Egypt was well-known for its wax-dyed cloth. This technique later spread through the Silk Road to Persia, India, China, Thailand, and Malaysia and eventually reached

Japan. The earliest physical evidence supporting this theory dates back to around the 5th to 6th centuries AD.

Another theory is the Indian hypothesis. According to some scholars, the wax-dyeing technique originated in India about 2,500 years ago. By the 5th century AD, it had spread westward to Egypt via Persia and reached China by the 7th century, later spreading to Japan and the Malay Archipelago. Other scholars believe that Indian batik was introduced to the western frontiers of China as early as the Eastern Han Dynasty (AD 25–220). Evidence supporting this theory includes a wax-dyed cotton cloth depicting a semi-nude female figure unearthed from a Han Dynasty tomb in Minfeng, Niya, Xinjiang. The figure, with arched eyebrows, a high nose, and deep-set eyes, is depicted with a plump face and body, bare breasts, and a necklace, holding a horn-like object with grain-like patterns at the top. This image may represent a goddess revered in Central and Western Asia, possibly with connections to Indian cultural elements, suggested by the halo behind her head.

A third hypothesis is the Malay Archipelago theory. Some scholars argue that batik originated in the Malay Archipelago, including Sumatra, Java, Borneo, and the Spice Islands. In Java, the wax-dyeing craft, known as batik, is a unique technique used to make large shawls. It first became popular among the islands of the Malay Archipelago before spreading to the Asian mainland. In the 16th century, Dutch and Portuguese traders in Java, especially with the establishment of the Dutch East India Company, helped spread the wax dyeing technique worldwide.

The fourth hypothesis is the Chinese theory. Some scholars maintain that dyeing had already become an important national industry in China as early as the Western Zhou period (1046–771 BC). By the Qin and Han dynasties (221 BC–AD 220) at the latest, ethnic minorities in southwest China were using beeswax and white wax to create blue and white patterned cloth. Therefore, in terms of using beeswax and white wax, China predates Egypt and India by several hundred years, indicating that the origin of batik is in China. In the 1960s, fragments of wax-dyeing artifacts dating from the Warring States to the Western Han period were discovered in a cliff tomb in Fengxiang Gorge, Fengjie County, Sichuan Province, providing the strongest physical evidence for the theory that wax-dyeing originated in China.

However, based on literary records and archaeological data, it is evident that the Han, Wei, Jin, and Southern and Northern Dynasties periods were undoubtedly when wax-dyeing technology matured and significantly developed. During this era, ethnic minorities in the southwest region utilized beeswax and paraffin as resist materials to produce fabrics with blue backgrounds featuring white or light-colored floral patterns, known as "Langan spot cloth." Texts from the Han Dynasty record that the descendants of Panhu, a figure revered as an ancestral deity by the Miao, Yao, and She ethnic groups in the southwest, wove bark fabrics and dyed them with plant seeds to create garments favored in five colors, embodying the vibrant "Langan spot cloth" style. Since these fabrics were mainly produced in Miao and Yao areas, they were also referred to as "Yao spot cloth." The Tang poet Liu Yuxi's *Barbarian Child's Song*, with verses like "the Barbarian language sings, and their clothes are vividly patterned," indicates that this custom of clothing, formed during the Han Dynasty, continued to be passed down. Archaeological finds of wax resist dyeing artifacts from this period are scarce and have mostly been discovered in Xinjiang. In addition to the wax resist dyed cotton cloth from a Han Dynasty tomb in Minfeng, Niya, additional finds include two pieces of blue woolen fabric with wax resist patterns from the Northern Dynasties period unearthed at the Wuyulaike ancient city site in Yutian County, Xinjiang, and a piece of blue wax resist dyed silk from the Western Liang period (AD 400–421) found in the Astana tombs in Turpan. One of the items from Wuyulaike features a pattern of small flowers with seven petals arranged into diamond-shaped grids, each with seven larger flowers; the other is decorated with small dots separating two flowers in an orderly pattern. The piece from the Astana tombs consists of patterns formed by small seven-petal flowers and straight rows of dots.

During the Sui, Tang, and Five Dynasties periods, products featuring wax resist dyeing were extremely popular, with varieties including cotton, wool, and silk. This era witnessed a significant expansion in the color palette, moving beyond the traditional blue and white to incorporate a wider range of hues for more complex dyeing. Artifacts from this time display colors like blue, yellow, brown, ochre, and green. Furthermore, the use of this art form extended to various applications, from everyday clothing and household items to military uniforms and interior decorations. Numerous artifacts of the Tang Dynasty, predominantly utilizing this technique, were found in the Mogao Caves in Dunhuang and the Astana tombs in Turpan. Additionally, Japan's Shosoin Repository preserves several contemporaneous pieces, including the intricate "Elephant under Tree" and "Sheep under Tree" screens. These items are notable for their detailed patterns and well-organized designs across their upper, middle, and lower sections, exemplifying the skilled craftsmanship of this dyeing method.

During the Song, Ming, and Qing dynasties, the traditional art of wax resist dyeing gradually diminished in the Central Plains region due to the widespread use of wax, its key material, leading to a scarcity of this resource. However, in the southwestern minority areas, where challenging transportation and limited technical communication coincided with an abundance of wax resources, this craft not only continued to thrive but also evolved with new techniques. The intricate processes and practices of wax resist dyeing in these minority regions were extensively documented in contemporary literature. For instance, Zhu Fu's *Ximan Congxiao* (*Tales from the Creek Barbarians*) from the Southern Song Dynasty vividly describes, "The people of Xitong deeply cherished bronze drums, more so than gold and jade, imitating their patterns by carving wax onto boards for fabric printing. The cloth was then dyed in indigo vats, in a method known as the 'dot wax technique.'" This passage highlights the Dong people's reverence for bronze drums and their unique method of using "dot wax" to imprint drum patterns on textiles, a testament to their rich cultural heritage. A blue-ground white-flower skirt of the Song Dynasty discovered in Tianxing Cave, Changshun County, Guizhou, in 1987 was analyzed to be created using this dot wax method. Zhou Qufei's *Lingwai Daida* (*Responses from the Region beyond the Mountains*) from the Southern Song Dynasty also recorded a cost-saving tie-dyeing technique, "Using two wooden boards carved with fine flowers to clamp the cloth, pour melted wax into the carvings, then release the boards and dye the cloth in indigo. After dyeing, the cloth is boiled to remove the wax, resulting in extremely fine flower patterns." In terms of craftsmanship, wax painting and dyeing are two crucial steps in wax resist dyeing. Wax painting generally involves hand-drawing wax patterns on fabric with a bamboo pen or wax knife, with the wax pattern disappearing and unrecoverable after melting during dyeing, making it a one-time process. Carving patterns on boards and then pouring wax into the carvings to form wax patterns allows for the repeated use of the pattern board, significantly saving wax painting time and reducing costs. It is economical and suitable for mass production of identical patterns. The Ming Dynasty's *Jiajing Tujing* (*Atlas of the Jiajing Period of the Ming Dynasty*) records, "The Miao women in southwestern China paint wax resist dyed flower cloth." The *Guizhou Tongzhi* (*Gazetteer of Guizhou Province*) also notes, "In the region, Miao women use wax-painted cloth for their skirts, with bright and colorful patterns," indicating that wax resist dyeing was an essential part of Miao women's daily life and clothing. As time passed, traditional wax resist dyeing methods and customs were still preserved in minority regions such as Guizhou, Yunnan, Guangxi, and Sichuan. Comparing their wax resist dyed products with unearthed artifacts reveals the development and evolution of wax resist dyeing techniques and culture.

2.2 The Craft of Wax Resist Dyeing

The wax resist dyeing process can be divided into several steps: fabric preparation, layout and positioning, wax melting, wax painting, dyeing, and wax removal and rinsing.

Fabric preparation: To facilitate wax painting, fabrics are often tentered and calendered to make them taut and smooth. Modern methods used by minority women include bleaching the self-produced cloth with grass ash and washing it clean, then applying a paste made from boiled konjac or bistort root juice evenly on the back of the fabric. After drying, the cloth is smoothed and polished with a smooth cow horn or stone, making it tentered and flat. Denser and smoother fabrics can skip this step.

Layout and positioning: The design is conceptualized beforehand, and then the pattern is positioned on the fabric according to the needs of the final garment. Skilled wax painters often do not need to sketch the design in advance; they may lightly draw large patterns with a pen on the fabric before boldly proceeding. For simplicity, some women use templates to outline patterns.

Wax melting: As wax is solid at room temperature, it must be melted into liquid before painting. This is done by heating the wax in a small copper pot or iron spoon over a charcoal fire. The wax used is usually paraffin or beeswax. Paraffin, a synthetic mineral wax, melts at 58°C–62°C and has low viscosity, making it prone to crack during dyeing and easy to remove. Beeswax, a yellow transparent solid extracted from beehives, melts at 55°C–62°C, has higher viscosity, and is less likely to crack, making it better for drawing lines. Some regions, like the White Trouser Yao people in Guizhou, use tree sap as a resist material, which they extract from a tree they call a "sticky paste tree." This tree undergoes a physical change in shape after sap extraction, appearing club-shaped, unlike unharvested trees, which look normal (Figure 1.21).

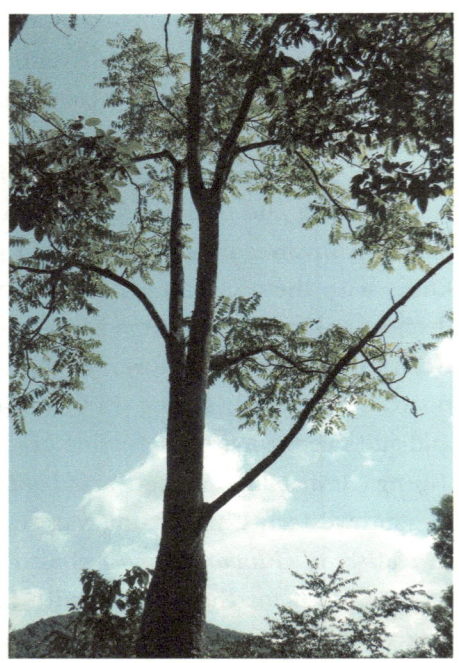

Figure 1.21 Sticky paste tree

Wax painting: A sharpened bamboo pen can be used for painting, but copper wax knives are more commonly used because the wax solidifies quickly when dipped. These wax knives vary slightly across regions but share fundamental similarities (Figure 1.22). The knife's edge is usually curved and made of double or multiple layers of brass with gaps in between. The best are made of brass. After dipping, the wax liquid stays between the copper layers and is applied to the fabric upon contact. This step is crucial

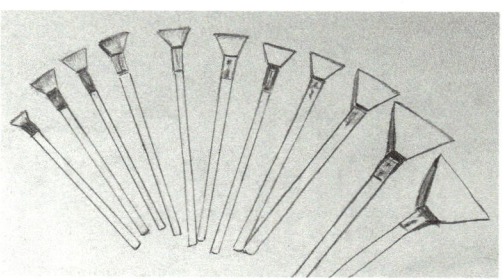

Figure 1.22 Wax knives

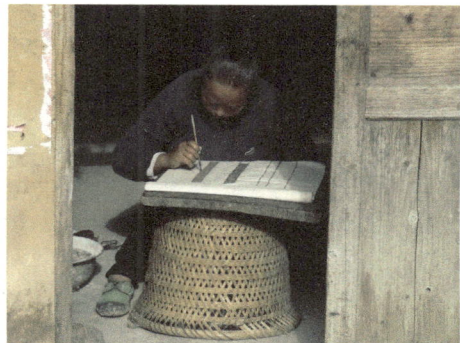

Figure 1.23 Wax painting

in wax-dyeing, not only determining the beauty of the pattern but also the success of the resist. The temperature of the wax liquid must be carefully controlled; if it is too hot, the wax will spread, affecting the smoothness and uniformity of the lines; if it is too cold, the wax will solidify quickly on the cloth without resisting the dye. Another critical skill is mastering the angle of the wax knife to create smooth, round, full, and elastic straight and curved lines, as well as to dot out round, semi-circular, and other patterns. Also, the speed and pressure of wax painting are important. Although copper wax knives can maintain the temperature of the wax liquid, any hesitation or pause will cause the wax to flow into a pool, affecting the smoothness and uniformity of the lines. After wax painting, the cloth is usually fixed on a platform or bamboo hoop to prevent the folding and cracking of the wax, which can lead to unwanted ice patterns and affect the overall effect of the design (Figure 1.23).

Dyeing: Before immersing the fabric in the dye vat, it needs to be soaked in water to even color. Taking indigo dyeing as an example, after soaking and draining the water from the fabric, it is shaken loose and slowly placed into the indigo vat, gently stirred, and dyed for 20–30 minutes. The fabric is then removed for sufficient oxidation in the air before being re-dyed in the vat. This process is repeated several times until the desired color is achieved. Lighter shades require fewer dips, while darker shades may need seven to eight or even ten dips. Before the final few dyes, bean paste may be brushed on to enhance the dye's adherence. A small corner of the fabric can be twisted to check the dyeing effect during the process. If the color in the twisted area does not lighten, it indicates that the fabric has been evenly dyed; if the color fades, it means further dyeing is needed.

Wax removal and rinsing: The fabric is soaked in boiling water and constantly agitated after dyeing. The hot water gradually melts the wax, separating it from the

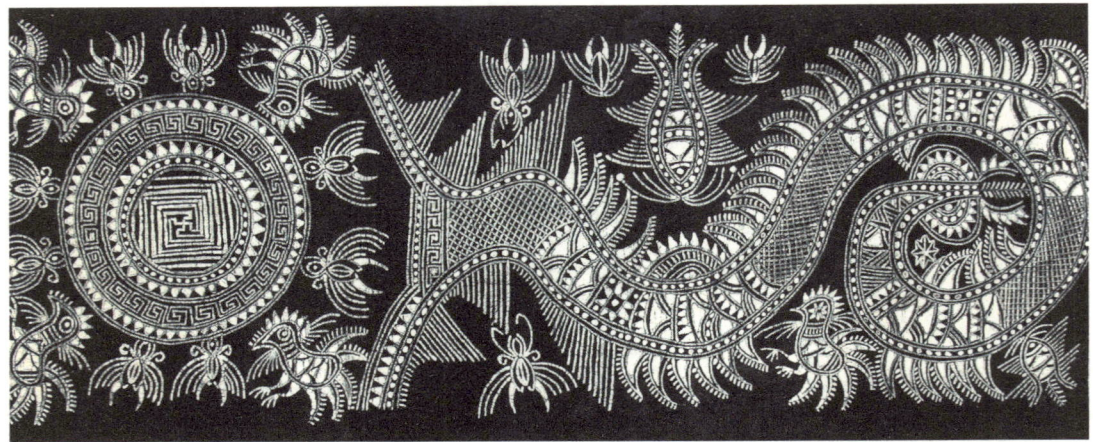

Figure 1.24 Wax resist dyed fabrics

fabric. Once the wax is removed, revealing the patterns, the fabric is lifted, rinsed in clean water to eliminate residue and excess dye, and dried. With this, the entire wax-dyeing process is completed (Figure 1.24).

2.3 Appreciation of Wax Resist Dyeing Artifacts

As a traditional Chinese handicraft, wax resist dyeing embodies meticulous craftsmanship and unique patterns, carrying rich historical and cultural connotations. Its delicate emotional expression and distinctive product aesthetics highlight the artistic charm of handicrafts, irreplaceable by modern printing and dyeing techniques. Below are some representative ancient wax resist dyeing artifacts.

The wax-dyed cotton cloth (Figure 1.25) is housed in the Museum of Xinjiang Uygur Autonomous Region and was excavated from the Eastern Han Dynasty tombs in Niya, Minfeng, Xinjiang. This Eastern Han wax-dyed artifact serves as a crucial piece of evidence supporting the origin of wax dyeing in India. However, the artifact itself, with remnants of a human foot, a segment of a lion's tail, and a lion's paw at its upper end, and images of a long dragon and flying birds at its lower end, showcases traditional Chinese auspicious patterns. This indicates that it is a product of cultural

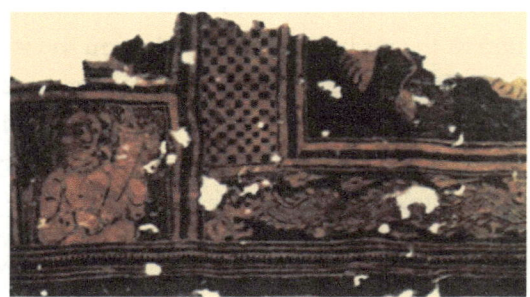

Figure 1.25 The wax-dyed cotton cloth of the Eastern Han Dynasty

exchange, embodying rich historical connotations. This wax-dyed piece is not only a rare domestic example of early Buddhist-themed imagery but also the earliest cotton fabric specimen discovered to date, making it exceptionally precious.

The blue wax-dyed woolen fabric of the Northern Dynasties period (Figure 1.26) is found at the Wuyulaike ancient city site in Yutian County, Xinjiang, and is preserved at the Museum of Xinjiang Uygur Autonomous Region. Its pattern consists of small flowers with seven petals forming diamond-shaped grids, each containing seven larger flowers. It was likely created using a dotting method, where a relief-patterned dotting tool is dipped in wax and applied to the fabric. The tool typically has circular points, with each type carved into a row, a circle of dots, or even a small flower made of dots. This technique later spread to the southwest of China, as evidenced by cotton fabrics and dotting tools found in Pingba County, Guizhou Province, and other sites, indicating further development of the dotting method in these minority regions.

The blue wax-dyeing silk of the Western Liang period (Figure 1.27) is from the Astana tombs in Turpan, housed in the Museum of Xinjiang Uygur Autonomous Region. Its clear wax patterns and even dyeing, similar in style to the Northern Dynasties period blue wax-dyed woolen fabric found in Yutian, suggest that geometric patterns or floral motifs composed of geometric shapes were prevalent in Xinjiang during this period.

The "Sheep under Tree" batik screen of the Tang Dynasty (Figure 1.28) is from the Shosoin Repository in Japan. This piece is printed on light yellow silk fabric, featuring hues of tea yellow and light green. The design centers around sheep and trees, enhanced by small hills, grass, and two monkeys. The depiction

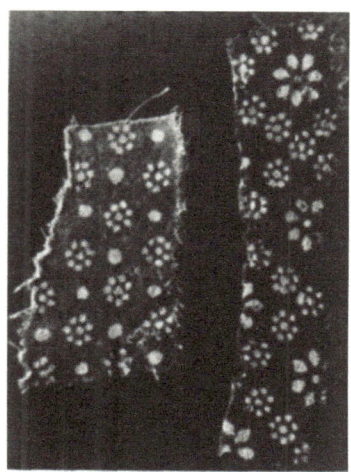

Figure 1.26 The blue wax-dyed woolen fabric of the Northern Dynasties period

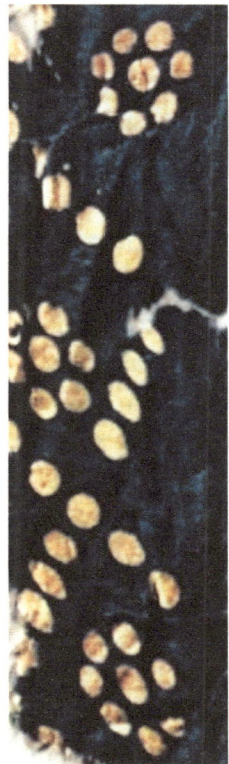

Figure 1.27 The blue wax-dyeing silk of the Western Liang period

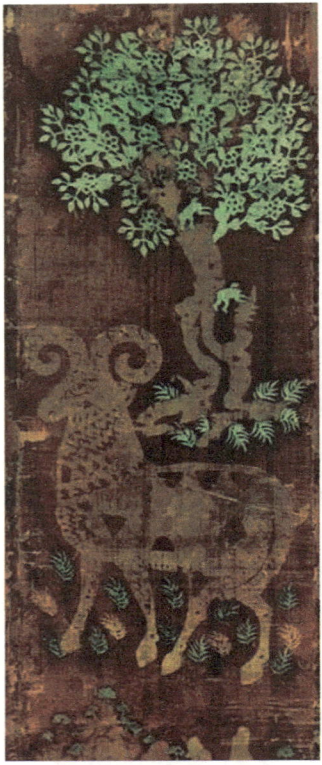

Figure 1.28 The "Sheep under Tree" batik screen of the Tang Dynasty

of the sheep is remarkably realistic, particularly the curved horns, which are vividly portrayed. The leaves on the tree, the two monkeys, and the grass on the ground are dyed green, bringing the scene closer to reality. The small hills at the bottom, disproportionate to the sheep and trees, employ a common technique in ancient Chinese painting to draw attention to the main subjects. In ancient China, sheep were seen as symbols of auspiciousness, representing harmony.

Also from Japan's Shosoin Repository, the "Elephant under Tree" wax-dyeing screen of the Tang Dynasty (Figure 1.29) is printed on a coarser light yellow silk fabric and features an elephant and tree as the main subjects, with small hills, grass, and a monkey, similar in composition to the "Sheep under Tree" screen. In China, elephants are also seen as auspicious, symbolizing the renewal and rejuvenation of all things.

The heron-patterned colored pleated skirt of the Song Dynasty from Guizhou Provincial Museum was found in Tianxing Cave, Changshun County, Guizhou (Figure 1.30). With a pleated design, the skirt has a white linen waistband connecting to the skirt. The overall pattern adopts a horizontal segmentation layout, dividing the skirt into three decorative bands: the shoulder, the knee band, and the hem. These bands are separated by horizontal stripe patterns. The shoulder part features paired heron patterns, with swirl patterns filling the spaces around the birds, creating a compact structure. The knee band primarily consists of a smooth decorative band formed by swirling lines. The hem features alternating symmetrical patterns embroidered with vine and coiled motifs. The skirt's primary color is indigo blue, complemented by white, dark orange-yellow, moon white, and willow green patterns. The contrast between dark orange-yellow and indigo blue enhances the vividness of the colors. Overall, the skirt has a simple, bright, and lively appearance without being gaudy and possesses a strong ethnic character. The dyes used are largely derived from local materials such as indigo, gardenia, and bayberry juice, applied through dipping and partial painting techniques.

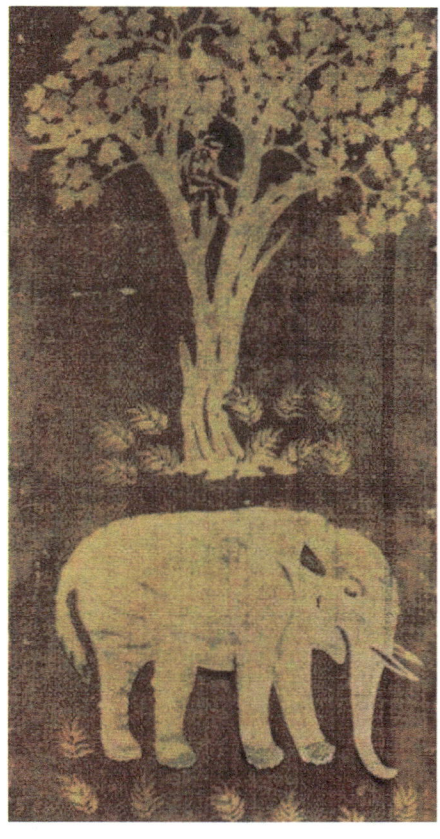

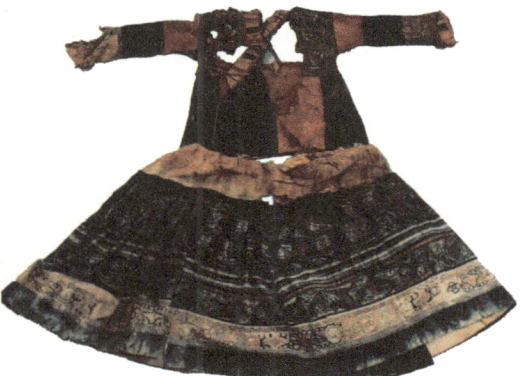

Figure 1.29 (LEFT) The "Elephant under Tree" wax-dyeing screen of the Tang Dynasty

Figure 1.30 (ABOVE) The heron-patterned colored pleated skirt of the Song Dynasty

The heron-patterned colored skirt of the Song Dynasty was discovered in a coffin cave in Pingba County, Guizhou, and is currently preserved at the Wax-Dyeing Cultural Museum in Anshun, located in Guizhou Province (Figure 1.31). The waist of the skirt is made from linen, while the body is crafted from cotton, featuring a blue background that highlights the colorful patterns. The craftsmanship includes color-filled wax-dyeing, drawn-work embroidery, and pieced cloth decorations. The wax-dyed patterns applied using the dotting technique are characterized by their smooth lines and realistic forms.

Figure 1.32 depicts a wax print of the "Panchang" pattern (the endless knot) from the Ming Dynasty (1368–1644). "Panchang" is one of the eight Buddhist

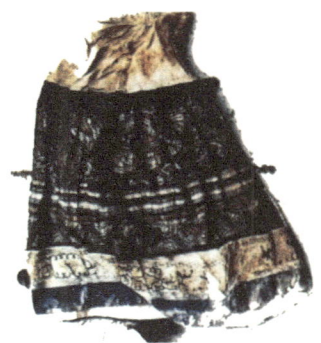

Figure 1.31 The heron-patterned colored skirt of the Song Dynasty

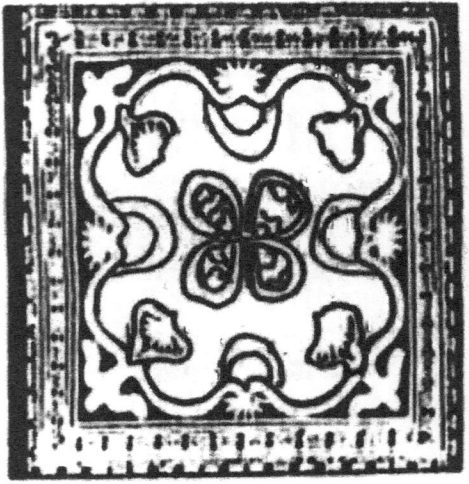

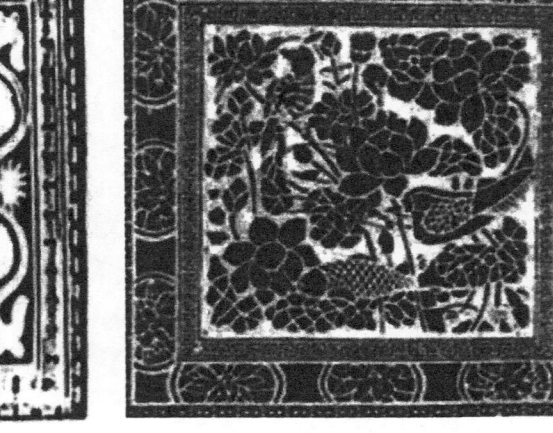

Figure 1.32 The wax print of the "Panchang" pattern (the endless knot) from the Ming Dynasty

Figure 1.33 The "Magpie, Lotus, and Carp" patterned artifact of the Qing Dynasty

treasures, known as "Ashtamangala" in Buddhism. These eight auspicious symbols, often used in Buddhism to signify good fortune, include the Conch Shell, Dharma Wheel, Precious Umbrella, Victory Banner, Lotus Flower, Vase of Great Treasure, Golden Fishes, and Panchang (the Endless Knot). They are collectively known as the "Eight Auspicious Symbols" or "Buddhist Eight Treasures." In the *Manual of the Buddhist Implements of the Yonghe Palace*, these eight treasures are explained as follows: The Conch Shell symbolizes the auspicious sound of the Dharma, spreading far and wide. The Dharma Wheel represents the teaching of the Buddha, turning endlessly across eons. The Precious Umbrella signifies protection and shelter for all beings. The Victory Banner represents the victory of Buddhist teachings over ignorance. The Lotus Flower symbolizes purity, emerging unsoiled from the muddy waters. The Vase of Great Treasure denotes the endless treasures of spiritual wealth and enlightenment. The Golden Fishes signify the courageous and lively spirit of liberation. "Panchang," or the Endless Knot, represents the interconnectedness of all things and the endless wisdom of the Buddha. Positioned eighth, it is commonly interpreted in folklore as a symbol of longevity, continuity, and unbroken progression. This wax print is natural in its depiction of wax drawing, with a vibrant and lively pattern.

Figure 1.33 shows a "Magpie, Lotus, and Carp" patterned artifact of the Qing Dynasty (1644–1911). Magpies, lotuses, and carps are popular auspicious patterns in Chinese folklore, symbolizing joyous events, many descendants, and academic success, respectively. This wax resist dyeing piece features delicate and smooth wax painting with a pattern that is full of vitality and life.

3. Clamp Resist Dyeing

Clamp resist dyeing is actually a form of resist dyeing using stencils. The process involves using two identically carved stencil plates. The fabric is folded and tightly sandwiched between these two plates. Then, various dyes are applied to the fabric either by dipping or injection, allowing the colors to be imprinted on the material. After the dyeing process is complete, the fabric is removed from the dye, and once the dye has dried, the stencil plates are then detached, revealing the corresponding patterns on the fabric. The ancient term *jiaxie* derives from this method of clamping and printing. For single-color *jiaxie*, generally, only one stencil plate is used. For multicolor *jiaxie*, multiple plates are required, with several colors being overdyed.

3.1 The Origin and Evolution of Clamp Resist Dyeing

There are three main perspectives on the emergence of clamp resist dyeing.

The first suggests its beginning in the Qin and Han dynasties. Liu Xiaosun of the Tang Dynasty, in his *Eryi Shilu* (*The Authentic Chronicles of the Two Principles*), records that clamp resist dyeing "originated during the Qin and Han periods, became commonly worn by all classes during the Chen and Liang periods, and was distinctly different in the palace of Emperor Wen of Sui."

The second perspective attributes its origin to the Sui Dynasty. Ma Gao of the Five Dynasties, in *Zhonghua Gujin Zhu* (*Annotations on Ancient and Modern China*), notes, "During the Daye period of Sui, Emperor Yang created five-colored floral gauze skirts of clamp resist dyeing for palace ladies and officials' wives and mothers."

The third viewpoint traces it back to the Tang Dynasty. Wang Dan of the Song Dynasty, in *Tang Yulin* (*Collection of Conversations in Tang Dynasty*), recounts, "Emperor Ming greatly esteemed his imperial consort, Liu Jieyu, for her scholarly talents. Jieyu's sister, who married into the Zhao family and was skilled in crafts, employed a technique of clamp-resist dyeing using carved boards. On the occasion of Jieyu's birthday, she presented a piece to Empress Wang. This piece was highly praised by the Emperor, who ordered its replication throughout the palace. Initially kept as a closely guarded secret, it gradually became widely known and was eventually adopted even by the less affluent."

Each of these views has its proponents and critics.

Proponents of the first viewpoint argue that the level of block printing technology during the Han Dynasty was highly advanced, as evidenced by the pattern-printed and dyed gauze, along with the gold and silver pattern-printed gauze, unearthed from the Mawangdui Han Tombs. Since clamp resist dyeing is a form of block dyeing, its emergence in the Han Dynasty is plausible. However, critics argue that *Eryi Shilu* often relies on interpretation and is not entirely trustworthy.

Proponents of the second view consider *Zhonghua Gujin Zhu* a reputable historical text, making its reliability unquestionable. Furthermore, the emergence of clamp resist dyeing in the Sui Dynasty is supported by the pattern of its dissemination and its popularity during the Tang Dynasty. Critics, however, note that only *Zhonghua Gujin Zhu* records this origin, and no clamp resist dyeing artifacts of the Sui Dynasty have been found, making the evidence for this view weak.

Proponents of the third viewpoint assert that the term "clamp resist dyeing" originated during the Tang Dynasty. This belief is based on the book *Tang Yulin*, which compiles a wide range of materials, including notes and stories from fifty scholars of the Tang Dynasty. It extensively documents the dynasty's political history, court affairs, scholars' conduct, literary anecdotes, customs, celebrated objects, and systems. *The Siku Quanshu Zongmu (The Complete Catalog of the Four Treasuries)* states, "While this book follows the narrative style of *Shishuo Xinyu (A New Account of the Tales of the World)*, it often aligns with official history in its recording of laws, historical facts, and exemplary words and deeds, differing from the more conversational style favored by Liu Yiqing." Furthermore, the account of clamp resist dyeing in *Tang Yulin* is detailed, with clear references to time, location, and characters, and is supported by a plethora of other literary records and archaeological findings. Critics, however, argue that the theory of the Tang Dynasty origin contradicts the patterns of emergence and spread of new crafts in ancient times. They point out that *Tang Yulin* largely replicates content from Zhao Lin's *Yinhua Lu (Compilation of Anecdotal Narratives)*, noting that Zhao Lin had a direct familial connection with the Zhao and Liu families, who are credited with inventing clamp resist dyeing. Additionally, the book's depiction of Liu Jieyu, a significant historical figure, greatly differs from official historical records, casting doubt on its objectivity and authenticity. Thus, it is often considered more a collection of legends than a credible historical source.

Although there is considerable debate over the origin of clamp resist dyeing, its refinement during the Tang Dynasty and its status as a high-end, fashionable dyed textile are indisputable facts. The technique is explicitly referenced in Bai Juyi's poems *Gift of Half-Bloomed Flowers to Langzhong Huangfu* and *Boating on Taihu Lake, a Letter to Wei Zhi*, as well as in Xue Tao's *Spring Outing and Gazing, Sent to Hermit Sun*. Moreover, actual clamp resist dyed items of the Tang Dynasty have been unearthed in tombs in Turpan, Xinjiang, and Dulan, Qinghai, although they are few in number. However, many sets of colored or monochrome items were discovered in the Dunhuang Library Cave (due to historical reasons, many of these items are now preserved in various museums across Europe). Several pieces are also kept in Japan's Shosoin Repository.) This evidence suggests that during the Tang Dynasty, clamp resist dyed products were already popular among the court and official classes, and were no longer considered rarities.

During the Five Dynasties and Song periods, clamp resist dyeing saw significant evolution and the introduction of new styles. One notable example from the Later Zhou Dynasty (AD 951–960) is the *zunzhong-xie*, a distinctive style featuring a black base with yellow flowers created by dyers in Kaifeng. Its uniqueness and high cost are highlighted by an incident where government official Chen Changda sold his prized musical instruments to acquire a tent trimmed with this fabric. Further evidence of the period's dyeing sophistication was found in a Northern Song printed scripture wrap with a light yellow double parrot pattern on a turquoise background, discovered in 1956 in the Huqiu Tower, Suzhou. This artifact is believed to have connections with the *zunzhong-xie*. In the same period, *mengjiachan* dyeing, characterized by a pattern of two large butterflies and created by a dyer named Meng in Kaifeng, gained significant popularity. Meanwhile, in Luoyang, *zhuanghua-xie*, created by a dyer named Li, became the market's favorite. *Zhuanghua* likely refers to a decorative flower technique akin to brocade patterning, suggesting these textiles mimicked brocade's colorful designs. Notably, *zunzhong-xie, mengjiachan*, and *zhuanghua-xie*, while not explicitly classified in historical records, are presumed to be clamp resist dyed products due to their intricate designs and premium pricing.

Despite the lower cost of producing high-end clamp resist dyeing compared to brocades, it was still expensive. The government in the Northern Song once decreed that clamp resist dyeing boards in Kaifeng should be strictly banned from production and trading to prevent its widespread popularity among the public. This ban was lifted in the early Southern Song period, leading to a resurgence in the production. Large dyeing workshops of the time could have dozens of flower boards for printing various types of products, often dyeing thousands of colored fabrics. The *Dongjing Menghua Lu (Memories of the Splendor of the Eastern Capital)* describes the grandeur of the fabric trading places in Lin'an, with transactions often reaching millions, which was astonishing. A Southern Song tomb in Shanxi unearthed a clamp resist dyeing Luo with a white paste hollowed-out pattern, demonstrating the high level of dyeing technology of the time.

By the Ming and Qing dynasties, simpler oil-paper hollowed-out dyeing began to prevail, and the production of clamp resist dyeing dwindled. However, the presence of clamp resist dyeing in Ming imperial tombs and the collections in the Palace Museum in Beijing indicate that clamp resist dyeing still held a certain position in Ming court textiles.

3.2 The Craft of Clamp Resist Dyeing

The process of clamp resist dyeing can be broadly divided into several steps: carving the boards, stacking and mounting the fabric, dyeing, removing the boards, and rinsing and drying.

Carving the boards: There are two types of clamp resist dyeing boards—raised pattern boards and hollowed-out boards, both carved from wood. Solid, fine-grained wood is used for carving larger areas with complex lines, while lesser-quality wood is used for simpler floral or bird patterns. Regardless of quality, the wood undergoes soaking, trimming, storing, smoothing, re-trimming, and sanding before carving.

The carving process for both raised and hollowed-out boards is similar. Initially, the envisioned pattern is drawn on paper and then transferred to the wood board. If an existing carved board is available, it can be used as a template to imprint the pattern onto a new board, similar to rubbings. During carving, small holes and grooves are created in closed areas of the pattern on the board to ensure smooth flow of the dye, with each board typically having at least ten small holes of 0.3 to 0.6 centimeters in diameter and several grooves for connectivity (Figure 1.34).

Stacking and mounting the fabric: The patterns on the clamp-dyed fabric are achieved by tightly clamping the fabric between carved dyeing boards, creating a resist-dye effect. The quality of the clamping process directly affects the outcome of the dyed pattern. Improper clamping can lead to the seepage of dye, causing colors from different areas to blend and affect each other, so this step is crucial. The method involves placing the folded fabric between the dye boards and aligning the edges of the fabric with the center of the boards. Iron frames are then fitted around the boards and tightened with wooden wedges. To prevent uneven dyeing due to fabric edges piling up, small hooks are attached to the frame using bamboo strips, allowing each edge of the fabric to be hooked up. This ensures even oxidation during dyeing and does not hinder the flow of dye within the boards, facilitating uniform coloring of the fabric's center.

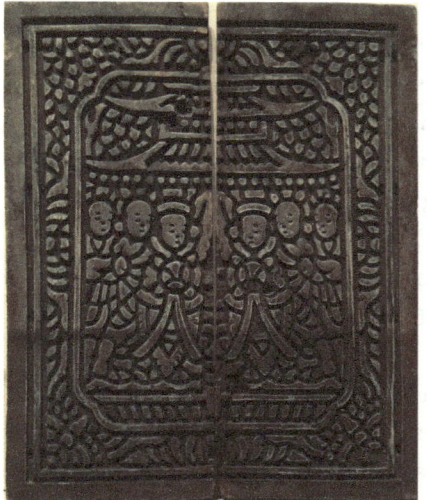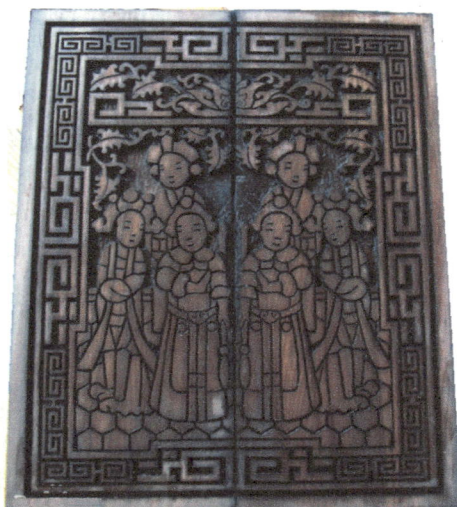

Figure 1.34 Dye boards

Dyeing: Dyeing techniques include two primary methods—immersion dyeing and injection dyeing. As per the expertise of Wu Yuanxin, a distinguished practitioner of this national intangible cultural heritage, the immersion dyeing method employs a clever use of leverage. This involves a bamboo pole, where one end is tied at a fifth of its length to suspend the weighty dyeing boards. The other end is adjusted with ropes and weights for control. The fabric block, prepared for clamp dyeing, is horizontally placed and secured to an iron frame, which is then hung from the pole's hook. The operator lifts the opposite end of the pole, immersing the frame and boards into a dye vat. This submersion is repeated every thirty minutes. After each immersion, the boards are rested on a wooden rack and shaken. This action allows the dye from the center of the boards to drain through the holes, facilitating the oxidation and gradual deepening of color on the fabric. The process is typically repeated 6 to 8 times until the desired color intensity is achieved. Injection dyeing, on the other hand, is commonly used for multicolored clamp dyeing. It involves the use of two identically patterned boards, which are mirror images of each other, clamping the fabric firmly. Color is then injected into specific holes as required by the design. If only a few sections need different colors, these areas are dyed first. Afterward, the holes are plugged with wooden wedges, and the whole board is submerged in the dye vat. With hollow-pattern boards, several boards featuring identical and completely open patterns are used to clamp the fabric. The areas in contact with the boards remain undyed. During the dyeing process, different colors are injected into the various sections of the hollow

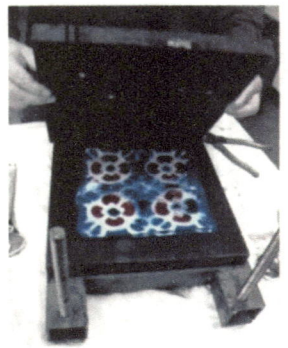

Figure 1.35 Dye boards removing (from the *Traditional Chinese Folk Printing and Dyeing Techniques* authored by Wu Yuanxin)

pattern, allowing the dye to penetrate the fabric. Following the initial dye application, other colors can be introduced for additional layers of dyeing.

Removing the boards: After dyeing, the boards clamped with fabric are removed from the dye vat and disassembled (Figure 1.35).

Rinsing and drying: The clamp-dyed fabric must undergo several rinses to remove excess dye and then hang on bamboo poles to dry.

3.3 Appreciation of Clamp Resist Dyeing Artifacts

Ancient clamp resist dyeing, known for its varied styles and delicate, vibrant colors, typically features patterns of flowers, birds, animals, and human figures. Most extant clamp resist dyeing artifacts were made during the Tang to the Five Dynasties period, with fewer examples from the Song Dynasty onwards, reflecting the gradual decline of this dyeing technique. Here are some representative pieces of ancient clamp resist dyeing.

The "Triangular Blue Floral Clamp-Dyed Banner" from the Tang Dynasty (Figure 1.36) is a piece discovered in the Dunhuang Library Cave and is now housed in the Victoria and Albert Museum in London. The banner is triangular in shape, with its body showcasing a petite floral clamp-dyeing technique. The design comprises a continuous pattern of flowers and leaves arranged in a square formation.

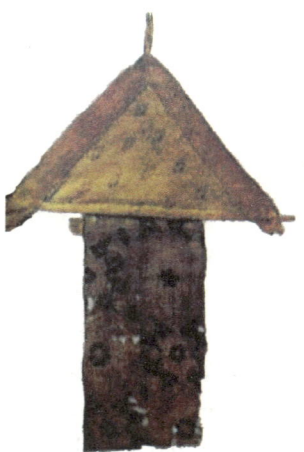

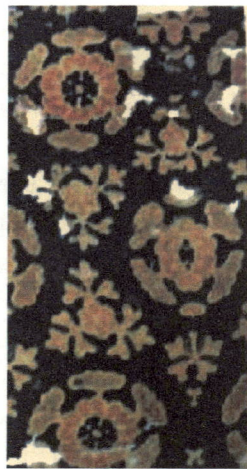

Figure 1.36 (FAR LEFT) Triangular Blue Floral Clamp-Dyed Banner from the Tang Dynasty

Figure 1.37 (LEFT) Blue Ground Floral Clamp-Dyed Silk of the Tang Dynasty

The "Blue Ground Floral Clamp-Dyed Silk" of the Tang Dynasty (Figure 1.37) is discovered in the Dunhuang Library Cave. This piece is currently housed in the Victoria and Albert Museum in London. Made on silk, the pattern features full-bodied floral clusters, interspersed with six-leaf designs, and smaller floral motifs in between, arranged in a spacious and bright layout. This clamp resist dyeing required three different boards for dyeing the background, flowers, and leaves. The holes in the wood boards were strategically placed to dye different parts of the pattern. The fabric was dyed in three stages to achieve the deep blue background, green leaves, and orange-red flowers.

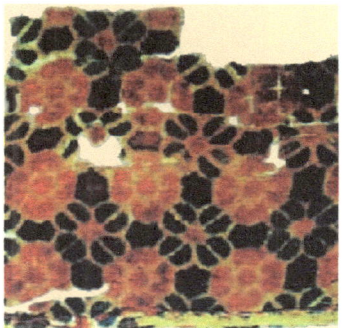

Figure 1.38 Red Flower and Green Leaf Clamp-Dyed Silk of the Tang Dynasty

The "Red Flower and Green Leaf Clamp-Dyed Silk" of the Tang Dynasty (Figure 1.38) is another artifact from the Dunhuang Library Cave, currently housed in the Victoria and Albert Museum in London. The pattern consists of four petals and four leaves as a unit, with many such units forming the complete design. The distinctive appeal comes from the red flowers and green leaves dyed on a yellow silk base.

From the Musée Guimet in Paris, the "Blue Ground Floral Pattern Clamp-Dyed Fabric" of the Tang Dynasty found in the Dunhuang Library Cave, features a blue base with green leaves and Baoxiang flowers, large and full-bodied (Figure 1.39). The blue ground was dyed first, followed by separately dyeing the green leaves and red parts.

As a part of the Hermitage Museum collection, the "Clustered Flower and Paired Deer Clamp-Dyed Banner" of the Tang Dynasty from the Dunhuang Library Cave features flower clusters surrounding deer amongst trees (Figure 1.40). This dyeing used two primary colors: orange-yellow for the background and blue for the deer, trees, and cluster frames. The flowers on the cluster ring alternate between brown-blue and bright blue due to color overlap.

The "Floral and Geese Motif Clamp-Dyed Silk" of the Tang Dynasty is another piece from the Dunhuang Library Cave (Figure 1.41). This clamp resist dyeing silk, measuring between 24 and 26 centimeters, consists of three pieces: two in the British Museum and one in the Hermitage Museum. Sewn into a triangular pennant, the complete pattern features a blue ground with a central circle of peonies and eight flying wild geese, surrounded by sixteen flowers forming the outer frame.

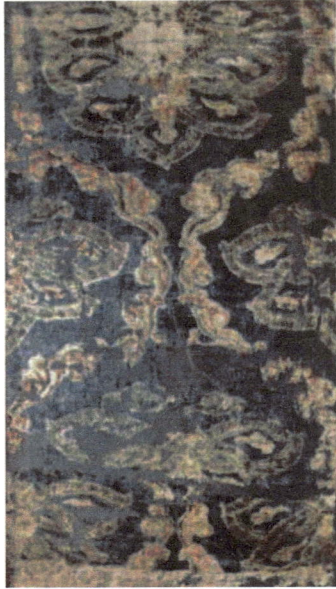

Figure 1.39 Blue Ground Floral Pattern Clamp-Dyed Fabric of the Tang Dynasty

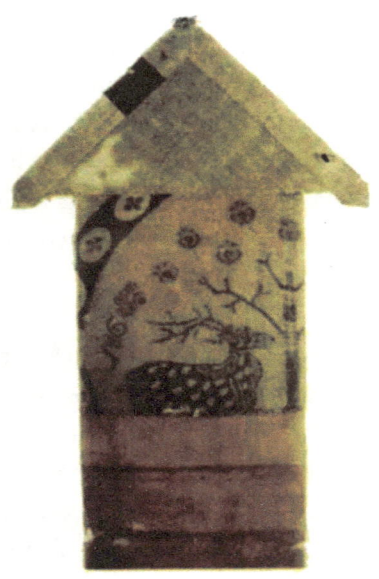

Figure 1.40 Clustered Flower and Paired Deer Clamp-Dyed Banner of the Tang Dynasty

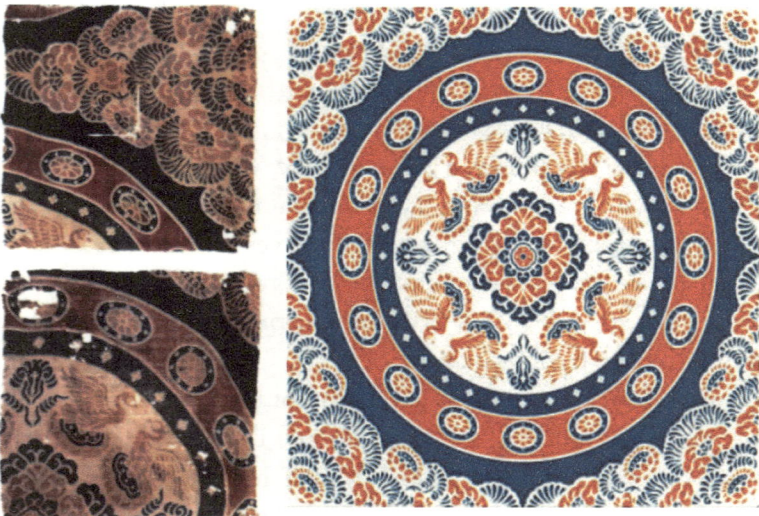

Figure 1.41 Floral and Geese Motif Clamp-Dyed Silk of the Tang Dynasty

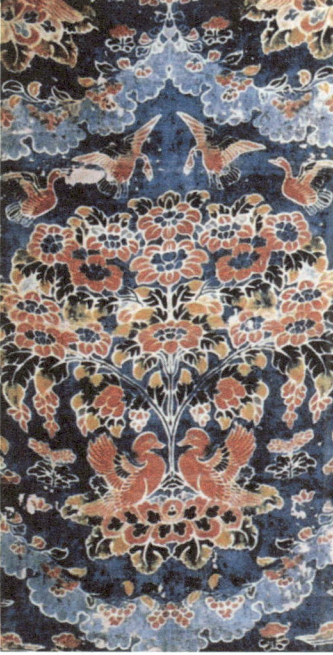
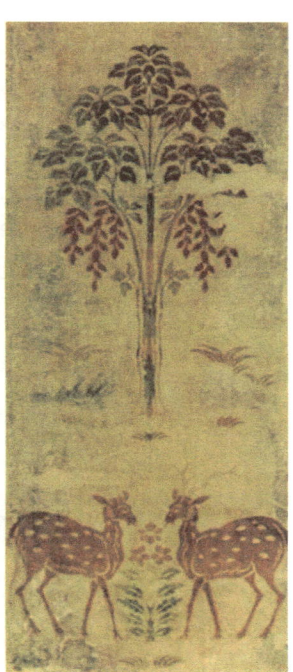

Figure 1.42 (RIGHT) Dark Blue Ground with Floral and Twin Birds Clamp-Dyed Silk of the Tang Dynasty

Figure 1.43 (FAR RIGHT) Pair of Deer Pattern Clamp Resist Dyeing Screen of the Tang Dynasty

The "Dark Blue Ground with Floral and Twin Birds Clamp-Dyed Silk" of the Tang Dynasty is from Japan's Shosoin Treasury (Figure 1.42). This clamp-dyed piece measures 104 centimeters in length and 53.5 centimeters in width, originally fashioned as a rectangular mat material. The pattern is set against a blue-dyed background, with the main motif being a blossoming tree on a lotus base. Between the tree and the lotus, there is a bird on each side, positioned as if about to take flight with wings spread. Above the tree are four birds, arranged in pairs facing each other, their wings fluttering as if in flight, interspersed with various colored floral patterns. During the dyeing process, the blue ground and parts of the flowers were first immersion dyed. Subsequently, the red patterns of the birds and flowers, as well as the green and yellow parts of the leaves, were added through injection dyeing.

Also from Shosoin, the "Pair of Deer Pattern Clamp Resist Dyeing Screen" of the Tang Dynasty (Figure 1.43) depicts a pair of relaxed deer under a tree, a popular theme in the Tang Dynasty, symbolizing harmony and prosperity. The dyeing process involved three stages: first the pale yellow ground, then the orange-yellow and green colors.

The "Floral, Tree, and Mountain Magpie Clamp-Dyed Screen" from the Tang Dynasty (Figure 1.44) is part of the esteemed collection at Japan's Shosoin. This

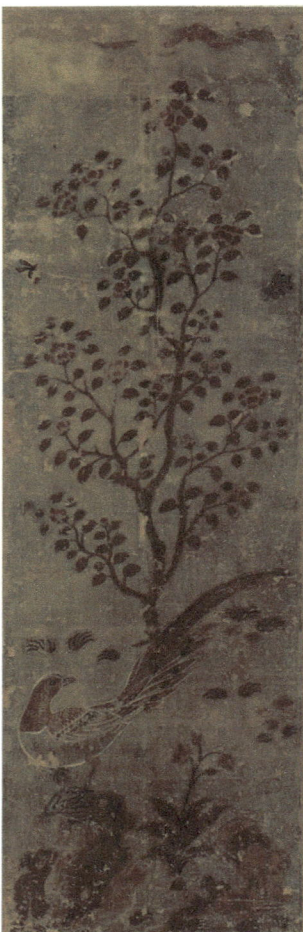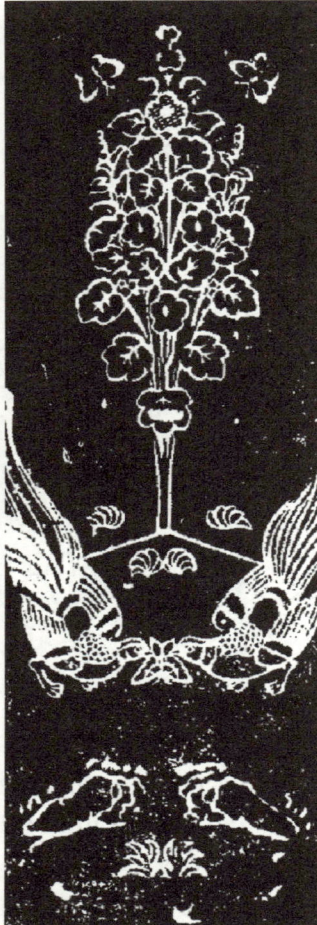

Figure 1.44 (FAR LEFT) Floral, Tree, and Mountain Magpie Clamp-Dyed Screen of the Tang Dynasty

Figure 1.45 (LEFT) Double Pheasant and Butterfly Clamp Resist Dyeing Screen of the Tang Dynasty (replica)

artistic piece is crafted on robust, pale yellow silk, skillfully dyed in hues of tea yellow and vibrant orange-red, with occasional splashes of blue-green. The design features a splendidly blooming tree under which a magpie, poised elegantly on a rocky outcrop, looks back with its tail gracefully upturned. The setting is further brought to life with an array of flowers, grass, and lively bees and butterflies in flight. As recorded in the Shosoin's *Catalogue of National Treasures*, this piece is part of a rare collection that includes nine sets of similar "Bird, Tree, and Stone Clamp-Dyed Screens," each consisting of six panels.

The "Double Pheasant and Butterfly Clamp Resist Dyeing Screen" from the Tang Dynasty (Figure 1.45) is a replica from Shosoin. The layout shows two pheasants competing for a butterfly under a flowering tree. The pheasants and flowers are depicted with lifelike detail, and the stones and grass beneath them are symmetrically arranged. The pheasant, a wild chicken with a white ring around its neck, was a regular pattern on ritual garments and popular in the Tang Dynasty decorative arts.

From the Museum of Indian Art in Berlin, the "Pair of Birds Clamp Resist Dyeing Silk" from the Tang Dynasty (Figure 1.46), is excavated in Turpan. This heavily damaged piece likely belonged to a larger clamp resist dyeing fabric. The surviving part features two opposing bird heads with decorative petal-like elements in a diamond shape. The dyeing process involved first coloring the red background and bird heads, then adding the blue bird eyes and diamonds.

The "Hunting Pattern Clamp Resist Dyeing Silk" of the Tang Dynasty (Figure 1.47) is from the Museum of Xinjiang Uygur Autonomous Region and was discovered in Turpan. The deep red silk features lively scenes of knights hunting lions, dogs chasing rabbits, and falcons pursuing birds, along with mountains and trees. The fabric was first dyed in the base color, then the pattern was added.

The "Silk Fragment with Blue Ground Floral Clamp Resist Dyeing" of the Tang Dynasty (Figure 1.48) is from the Qinghai Provincial Institute of Cultural Relics and Archaeology. This piece, consisting of two sewn-together fragments, has a blue ground floral design on top and a yellow ground folded branch pattern below. The first was dyed blue with red-brown flowers, while the second had a yellow base with separately dyed red and blue flowers.

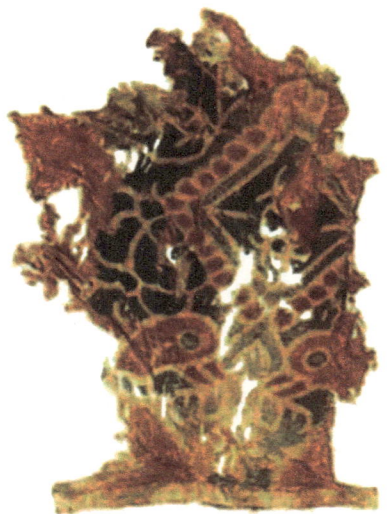

Figure 1.46 Pair of Birds Clamp Resist Dyeing Silk of the Tang Dynasty

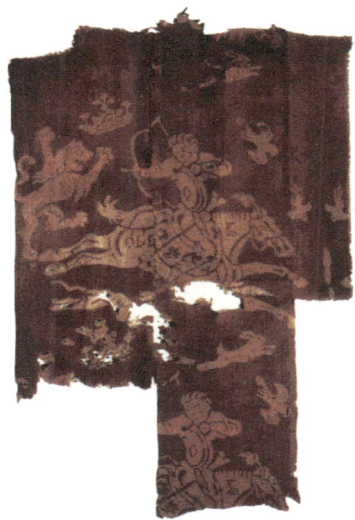

Figure 1.47 Hunting Pattern Clamp Resist Dyeing Silk of the Tang Dynasty

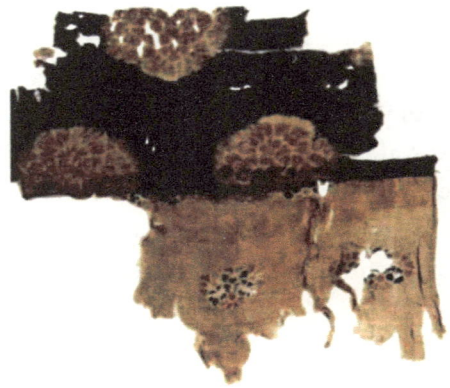

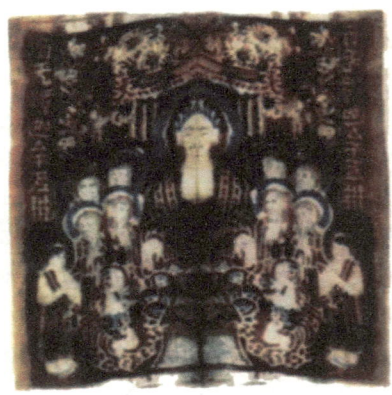

Figure 1.48 Silk Fragment with Blue Ground Floral Clamp Resist Dyeing of the Tang Dynasty

Figure 1.49 Namo Shakyamuni Buddha Image Clamp-Dyed Silk of the Liao Dynasty

The "Namo Shakyamuni Buddha Image Clamp-Dyed Silk" from the Liao Dynasty (Figure 1.49) is discovered in the wooden pagoda of the Fogong Temple in Ying County, Shanxi. This silk artifact, naturally yellow-toned, is dyed in red and blue. It is nearly square, 65.8 centimeters in height, and 62 centimeters in width. The depicted Shakyamuni Buddha is robed in red, with a red and blue halo around his head. Seated in a meditative pose on a lotus pedestal, his hands rest gently on his knees. Surrounding figures, shown in various colors, stand with hands pressed together in reverence. The canopy pattern above the Buddha is the auspicious Baoxiang flower. Around the outer edge, the phrase "南无释迦牟尼像" (Namo Shakyamuni Buddha Image) is printed in a unique style, with characters reversed on the left and correct on the right, indicating a double-fold dyeing technique. This representation of the Buddha in clamp-dyed silk is a unique example among existing ancient clamp-dyed artifacts.

The "White Ground with Lotus Clamp-Dyed Gauze" of the Liao Dynasty (Figure 1.50) is from the Baita Temple in Balinzuoqi, Chifeng, Inner Mongolia. The fabric was composed of four lotus flower boards, each with visible seeds, symbolizing fertility. It was folded in four and dyed using a single color.

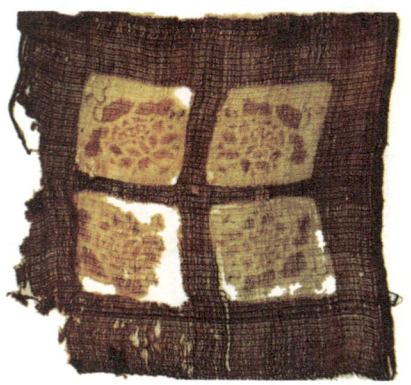

Figure 1.50 White Ground with Lotus Clamp-Dyed Gauze of the Liao Dynasty

As a private collection, the "Large Sleeve Robe" from the Yuan Dynasty features a blue-

and-white floral clamp resist dyeing lining (Figure 1.51). Despite the faded patterns, faint floral motifs and blue vines or bird patterns can still be discerned. The dyeing process involved folding and clamping the fabric between boards, dyeing the red base, and then selectively adding light floral, blue vine, or bird patterns. This unique piece represents the only known clamp resist dyeing artifact of the Yuan Dynasty.

The "Flowers and Fruits Multicolor Clamp Resist Dyeing Silk Handkerchief" of the Ming Dynasty, is housed in the Beijing Palace Museum (Figure 1.52). Measuring 55.5 centimeters in length and 56 centimeters in width, it features melons, pomegranates, radishes, eggplants, and

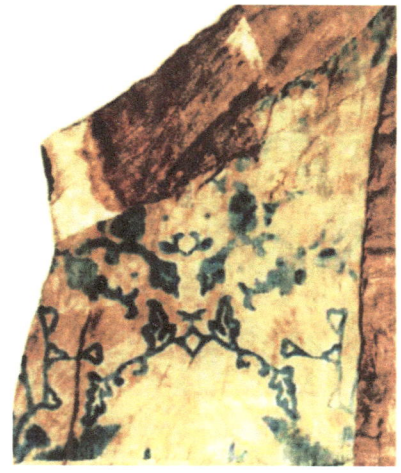

Figure 1.51 Large Sleeve Robe of the Yuan Dynasty

camellias in blue, white, red, yellow, and orange hues on a blue ground. The blue base was dyed first, followed by the addition of the other colors.

The "Multicolored Clamp-Dyed Silk Wrap with Fish and Lotus Pattern" of the Ming Dynasty is also from the Beijing Palace Museum (Figure 1.53). This piece is crafted from white plain silk without a dyed ground, measuring 50 centimeters in height and 55 centimeters in width. It features a pattern of lotus flowers with stalks,

Figure 1.52 Flowers and Fruits Multicolor Clamp Resist Dyeing Silk Handkerchief of the Ming Dynasty

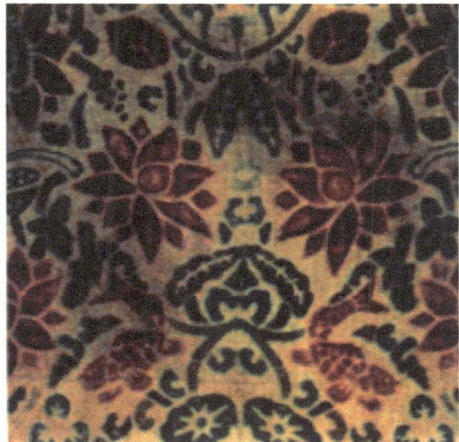

Figure 1.53 Multicolored Clamp-Dyed Silk Wrap with Fish and Lotus Pattern of the Ming Dynasty

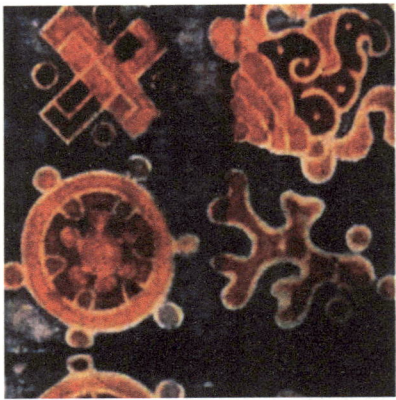

Figure 1.54 Multicolored Clamp-Dyed Silk Wrap with Auspicious Treasures

among which two lively golden fish are depicted playfully weaving in and out. The lotus flowers and fish are rendered in light red, while the lotus leaves and seed pods are in shades of green and blue. The pattern is symmetrically arranged around a central fold line, creating a mirror image on either side.

The "Multicolored Clamp-Dyed Silk Wrap with Auspicious Treasures" is from the Dingling tomb of the Ming Dynasty (Figure 1.54). It measures 55 centimeters in length and 44 centimeters in width and features the Eight Treasures pattern on a blue background.

4. Blue Calico Cloth

Blue calico cloth refers to a traditional Chinese indigo-dyeing craft that uses natural indigo extracted from *Indigofera tinctoria*. The process involves creating a resist paste with materials like lime and soybean flour. This paste is applied to the fabric to prevent dye absorption, resulting in designs where the treated areas remain white against a blue background. The craft is distinguished by its simplicity, purity, and harmonious blue and white color scheme. In terms of its technical aspects, blue calico cloth represents a physical resist-dyeing technique, where the paste blocks the dye to create patterns of blue-on-white (known as "*yin* print") or white-on-blue (called "*yang* print"). The cloth with patterns on one side is referred to as "front print," while cloth printed on both sides is called "double print." Blue calico cloth is relatively more cost-effective than other dyeing methods, but its practicality and artistic appeal have made it extremely popular among the common people since its inception. This popularity is reflected in its various local names across different regions of China: it's known as "Yaoban Cloth" (a type of fabric that has a pattern resembling medicine stains or spots) in Jiangsu, "Mahua Cloth" (a fabric pattern that resembles twisted or braided hemp) in the Northeast, "Douran Cloth" (fabric dyed with soybean flour) in Hubei, "Pattern Dyed" in Fujian, and "Cat's Paw Print" in Shandong, highlighting its widespread appeal.

4.1 The Origin and Evolution of Blue Calico Cloth

The origin of blue calico cloth, according to textile historians and references in the ancient compendium *Gujin Tushu Jicheng · Zhifang Dian* (*The Complete Collection of Illustrations and Writings from the Earliest to Current Times · Treatise on Administrative Geography*), is generally attributed to the "Yaoban Cloth" from the Southern Song Dynasty. The text states: "Yaoban Cloth originated from Jiading and Anting towns, created by a person named Gui during the Jiading era of the Song Dynasty. The cloth was made by smearing gray medicine and dyeing it blue." Another entry in the same book mentions: "Yaoban Cloth, commonly known as Jiaohua Cloth, is now found everywhere." There are several key reasons identified for the emergence of this new craft during this period.

Firstly, blue calico cloth is a craft that evolved from the already sophisticated techniques of tie-dyeing, wax-dyeing, and clamp-dyeing. These three dyeing methods laid the technical foundation for its coloring process. It can be produced using any of these three techniques, and the use of a "plate" or "board" is a common element in all of them. For instance, in clamp dyeing, two carved boards with the same pattern are used to tightly sandwich the fabric, creating resist patterns through the board's design. In wax dyeing, two hollowed wood boards are used to sandwich the fabric to save costs and facilitate mass production. The wax is then poured into the hollows, forming a resist and eventually producing wax-dyed fabric. Similarly, in tie-dyeing, small wooden boards are used to create patterns through a method of binding and twisting.

Secondly, the blue calico cloth's resist paste application was inspired by the traditional Chinese printing technique of rubbing. Rubbing, a traditional Chinese skill, has been widely used since at least the Spring and Autumn period and essentially involves intaglio printing technology. In ancient times, the fields of printing and carving were closely intertwined. For instance, *The Collected Works of Master Hui'an* lists the crimes of the corrupt official Tang Zhongyou, which included using official funds for carving printing boards for his collections of poems. Additionally, he was accused of exploiting his position to create carved boards for dyeing fabrics, producing dozens of pieces to be used in his family's dyed fabric shop. Therefore, the development of intaglio printing not only facilitated the emergence and advancement of rubbing but also stimulated the progression of dyeing block technology.

Thirdly, the method of paper-cutting provides a basis for the pattern design in the production of blue calico cloth. Fragments of paper-cutting from the Northern Dynasties period, featuring a group of horses and flowers motif, were unearthed at the Gaochang ruins in Turpan, Xinjiang, indicating that the technique of paper-cutting predates blue calico cloth. The design similarities between paper-cutting and the patterns used in blue calico printing, such as the blue-on-white or white-on-blue floral patterns, are strikingly similar to the negative and positive carving techniques in paper-cutting. From a logical perspective, the production of the patterns was very likely inspired by the art of paper-cutting.

Fourthly, the resist dyeing technique with lime paste has laid the groundwork for the synthesis of lime paste in blue calico production. As early as the Tang Dynasty, the resist paste, made from lime and wood ash, was already in use. Later, the paste for blue calico was made from soybean flour and other ingredients.

Fifthly, the dyeing ban during the Song Dynasty spurred the development of the blue calico craft. The dyeing bans issued several times during the Song Dynasty accelerated the decline of the "three dyeing methods," which were relatively complex and costly. In contrast, blue calico craft, which involves paper-based resist paste application, had a simpler process and easier material acquisition. It could produce patterns not inferior to "Sanxia," meeting the material needs and spiritual aspirations of the common people.

With the advent of the Ming and Qing dynasties, cotton fabric entirely supplanted hemp fabric as the predominant textile for the general populace. It became a common sight in everyday life because of its intense blue and pure white contrast, uniform and neat pattern outlines, simple and striking lines, and auspicious and festive designs. Workshops producing blue calico cloth sprang up across various regions, leading to a multi-faceted and comprehensive craft development, forming a well-established craft system. Historical documents record that in regions like Shandong and Jiangsu, where the production of cloth was advanced, there were specialized workshops and artisans dedicated to carving and selling printing blocks. The number of specialized workshops for smoothing the cloth was remarkably high, particularly in the Jiangnan area, with Suzhou being the most notable. In the 59th year of Emperor Kangxi's reign (1720), the number of people engaged in the foot-stomping cloth technique in and around Suzhou was over ten thousand. By the 8th year of Emperor Yongzheng's reign (1730), there were more than 450 workshops related to the technique in the Chongmen area of Suzhou alone, with over 10,900 foot-treadled stones, each workshop employing dozens of craftsmen. By the end of the Qing Dynasty, the production of blue calico cloth had reached an annual output of 600,000 *pi*. The main production areas included Jiangsu, Zhejiang, Hunan, Shandong, Henan, Hebei, Sichuan, Shanxi, Shaanxi, and the northeastern provinces, each developing its own unique style, with Jiangsu and Zhejiang being the most distinctive. According to Chu Hua's *Mumian Pu* (*The Annals of Cotton in Shanghai*) from the Qing Dynasty, the

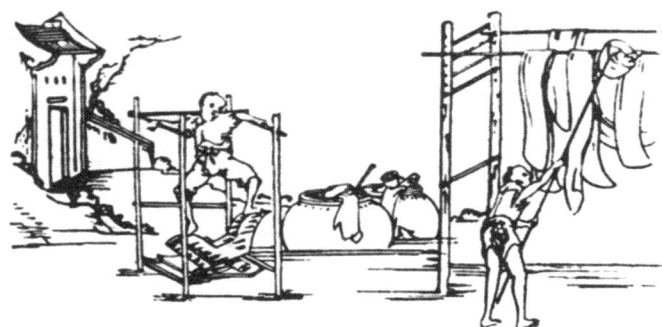

Figure 1.55 Traditional foot-stomping cloth technique in the late Qing Dynasty

process of smoothing the cloth involved rolling the fabric around a wooden shaft, placing it on a polished stone slab, and pressing it with a smooth, *yuanbao* (sycee)-shaped heavy stone, weighing about a thousand jin. A person would then step on both ends of the indentation and exert force back and forth to make the cloth tight, thin, and glossy (Figure 1.55).

4.2 The Craftsmanship of Blue Calico Cloth

The process of making blue calico cloth can be broadly divided into several steps: creating oil-paper boards, designing on the boards, making the printing boards, scraping the resist paste, dyeing, airing and scraping off the paste, washing and drying, and pressing.

Creating oil-paper boards: Select several sheets of tough paper or rice paper. Brush each sheet with wheat paste and mount them together, one by one. Allow them to dry on a wall or board surface. Once dry, peel them off and trim the edges to make them even. Then, apply a layer of tung oil or persimmon oil to enhance the paper's water resistance. After the oil has dried, press the paper flat for use. The ideal thickness of the finished paper board is about 2 millimeters.

Designing on the boards: To ensure the design's integrity, the pattern's characteristics are considered first to avoid breakage due to thin lines or leakage during scraping. Once the design is finalized, it's drawn onto the paper board with black ink. If there's a master template, it's directly printed onto the board, a process known as a "replacement board" in the industry.

Making the printing boards: Utilizing a specialized carving knife, the pattern is meticulously incised into a hollowed-out stencil following the designed draft. After the carving process, the plate is initially smoothed with a cobblestone, then repeatedly coated on both sides with cooked tung oil multiple times. During this oil application, precision in quantity is crucial. Excessive oil can alter the pattern or cause the board

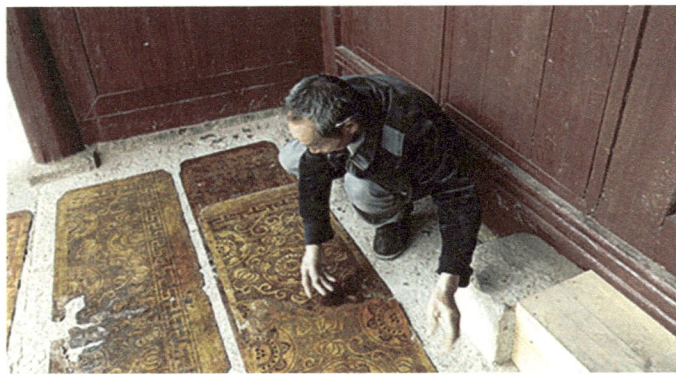

Figure 1.56 Printing boards

to be uneven. In contrast, insufficient oil fails to adequately permeate the paper core, reducing the board's durability and water resistance and subsequently diminishing its usability. Hence, the initial oil layer should be sparingly and thinly applied, followed by subsequent layers once dry. The completed, air-dried, and flattened board is then ready for use. Typically, printing blue patterns on a white base requires only a single board. However, for printing white patterns on a blue base, two distinct boards, termed the "primary board" and the "covering board," are essential (Figure 1.56).

Scraping the resist paste: The paste, optimally made from soybean flour and corn, wheat, or glutinous rice flour mixed with lime, is applied differently depending on the design background. For designs with a blue background, where only a single board is used, the fabric is first laid flat under the board and secured. The board is then placed on top, and the paste is evenly scraped through its open areas to adhere to the fabric. In contrast, white background designs require two applications of paste. The first is applied using the primary board. After this layer becomes semi-dry, the covering board, aligned with the initial pattern using specially carved marks for accuracy, is placed for the second application. Care must be taken to apply the paste at an optimal thickness: too thin, and it will spread, causing blurred edges; too thick, and it will not thoroughly penetrate the fabric, leading to incomplete patterns.

Dyeing: Before dyeing, the paste-applied fabric is first loosened and soaked in clean water until the fabric is wet and the paste softens. Then, it's ready to be dyed in the vat. The dye is made from plants like *Persicaria tinctoria* (Japanese indigo), *Isatis tinctoria* (woad), or *Strobilanthes cusia* (Chinese woad), with polygonum tinctorium being preferred. This preference is due to its medicinal properties of repelling insects and detoxifying, as mentioned in the *Bencao Gangmu* (*Compendium of Materia Medica*) by Li Shizhen. It notes that if one is injured by a poisoned arrow and immediate herbal remedies are unavailable, using a cloth dyed in this indigo to

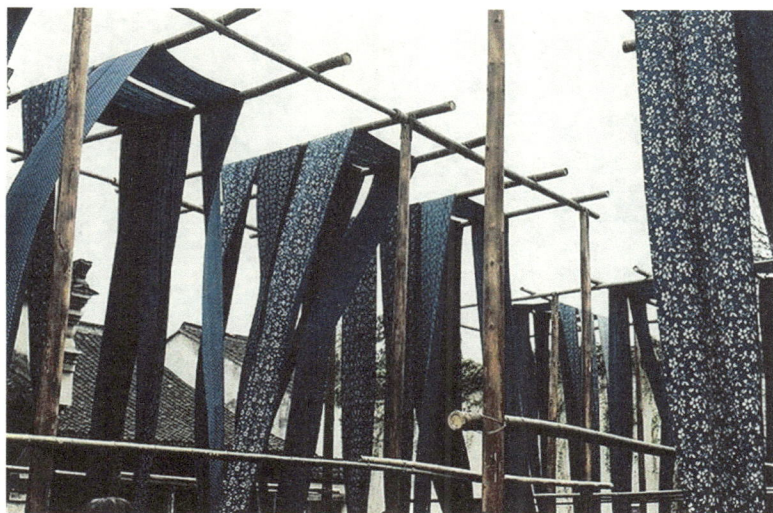

Figure 1.57 Drying the blue calico textile

absorb the juice can act as a detoxifier. Since indigo dyeing is generally done at room temperature, there might be some excess dye after washing. Multiple immersions in the dye vat may be necessary to achieve the desired color.

Airing and scraping off the paste: After dyeing, the fabric is hung to drip-dry over the dye vat and then aired on racks. It's best to choose sunny weather for drying to prevent mold. Once dry, the fabric is stretched and scraped to remove the surface paste.

Washing and drying: The fabric is then washed 2–3 times to remove any residual paste and excess dye. It is hung on a high rack (about 7 meters) to dry (Figure 1.57).

Pressing: After washing and drying, the fabric is smoothed and flattened using a stone roller, then either folded or rolled into bolts for future use.

4.3 Appreciation of Blue Calico Artifacts

With its striking blue hues and dazzling white, blue calico cloth boasts an elegance that transcends the ordinary and a lively grace. This fabric's unique cultural allure is defined by the natural texture created through the resist dyeing process and the patterns rich in stories and symbolism. Regrettably, due to the vulnerability of cotton to degradation, most surviving examples date back only to the late Ming and Qing dynasties, with earlier specimens yet to be found. Below is a brief overview of three blue calico quilt tops of the Ming Dynasty from the Minhang Museum in Shanghai and several pieces from the Ming and Qing periods at the Museum of Blue Calico Cloth in Nantong.

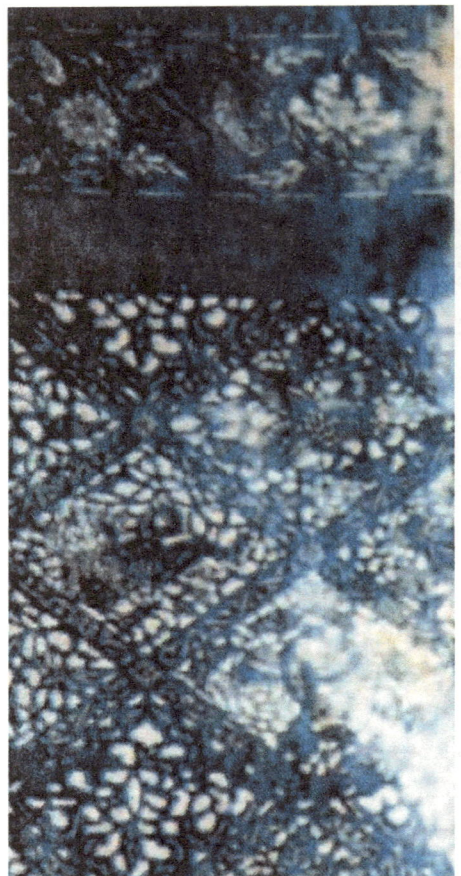

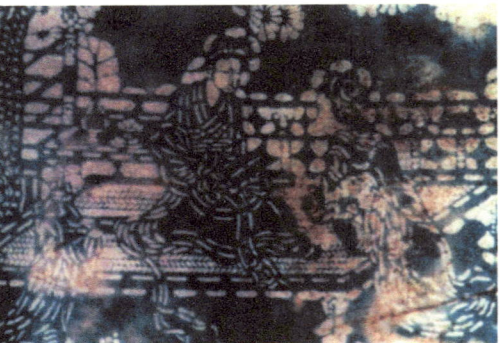

Figure 1.59 The "Courtyard Figure Pattern" quilt top of the Ming Dynasty (partial)

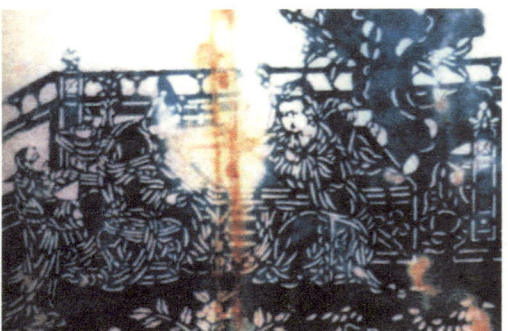

Figure 1.58 The "Diamond Skeleton Pattern" quilt top of the Ming Dynasty (partial)

Figure 1.60 The "Chess-Playing Courtyard Pattern" quilt top of the Ming Dynasty (partial)

Figures 58, 59, and 60 are the quilt tops unearthed in Maqiao Town. They feature a diamond skeleton pattern, a courtyard figure pattern, and a chess-playing courtyard pattern. Despite significant damage, these quilts offer a glimpse into their original intricacy.

The "Diamond Skeleton Pattern" quilt top measures 194 centimeters in length and 162 centimeters in width, consisting of three stitched segments. Each segment, 52 centimeters wide, features patterns of flowers, phoenix birds, and lions rolling embroidered balls within diamond grids. The quilt has wide blue margins at the top and bottom, decorated with phoenixes playing with peonies and chrysanthemum borders. The main pattern consists of continuous diamond grids, with each center four-grid set forming a group. In the top and bottom grids, there are phoenixes flying through peonies. The left and right grids contain lions rolling embroidered balls among floral patterns. The detailed and complex patterns, likely created using a set of scraping plates, display a rhythmic interplay of dots, lines, and planes in blue and white.

The "Courtyard Figure Pattern" quilt top measures 192 centimeters in length and 127 centimeters in width, assembled from three panels to form a complete design. It features a blue border at the top and bottom, measuring 33 centimeters and 31 centimeters, respectively, surrounded by a frame decorated with floral, bird, and lion playing with embroidered ball motifs. Below the upper border, a horizontal row of three apertures contains bird-and-flower branch patterns. The central theme showcases a tall pine and banana tree within a courtyard and gallery, where two noblewomen chatted on couches. Both women are elaborately dressed, with high hair buns adorned with hairpins, forehead bands, earrings, and other jewelry, draped in luxurious attire and shawls, each accompanied by a servant. The left side of the scene depicts mountains, trees, pavilions, and temples, with a rugged path winding down the mountain. Along this path, a mounted official and two servants carrying luggage walk, illustrating a serene moment as the women patiently await the official's return. The clarity and smoothness of the pattern lines on the front suggest skilled application of the paste, with an appropriate mixture and application thickness. Observing from the back, the paste's excellent penetration and resist properties are evident, likely due to the use of a sticky glutinous rice paste applied with a two-block printing process, indicating no significant crackling.

The "Chess-Playing Courtyard Pattern" quilt top measures 205 centimeters in length and 164 centimeters in width, with blue borders of 37 centimeters at the top and 41 centimeters at the bottom. The design features distant mountains and nearby water surrounding a courtyard scene, where the main focus is on two individuals engaged in a chess game, flanked by several maids on each side. The courtyard is a blend of galleries, winding paths, artificial mountains, streams, flowers, banana plants, and assorted trees. The backdrop of rolling hills outside the courtyard is depicted with extensive use of negative space. The gray paste and technique used are the same as those in the "Courtyard Figure Pattern" quilt top.

Figure 1.61 shows a restoration of the Qing Dynasty's "Phoenix Playing with Peony" quilt top pattern. The phoenix, king of birds, combined with the peony, king of flowers, creates a dynamic and rounded motif that not only symbolizes wealth, auspiciousness, and the vibrant yang energy of happiness and harmony but also ranks among the most beloved traditional auspicious patterns in Chinese culture. Widely used in the decoration of various textiles, ceramics, and wood items, the phoenix and peony pattern on this quilt top is characterized by its simplicity and delicate lines, with a clear distinction between blue and white.

Figure 1.62 is a restoration of the "Qilin Bringing Sons" quilt top pattern of the Qing Dynasty. The Qilin (Chinese Unicorn), a benevolent mythical creature in Chinese folklore, has been ranked alongside the dragon, phoenix, and tortoise as one of the "Four Auspicious Beasts" since the Zhou Dynasty, standing at the forefront as a symbol of peace and good fortune. Folk tales suggest that the appearance of a Qilin heralds auspicious events, bringing intelligent and lovely boys to virtuous families without heirs, thereby ensuring their prosperity and the continuation of their lineage for generations. As such, blue calico quilt tops depicting the theme were commonly seen among the festive items prepared for children's weddings in olden times. The main pattern of this quilt top, framed within a floral window, not only highlights the subject but also creates a harmonious balance between motion and stillness.

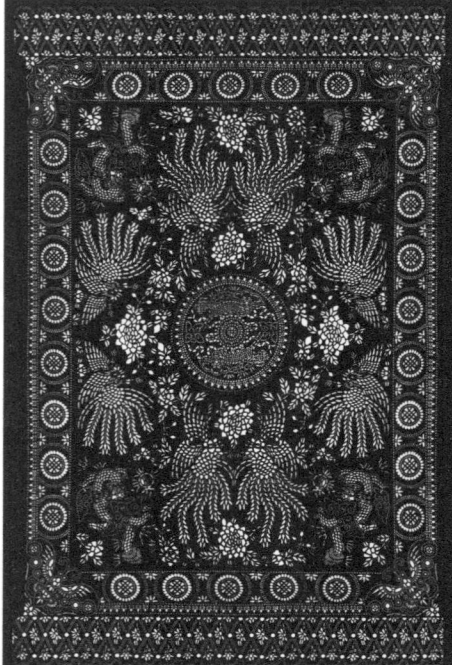 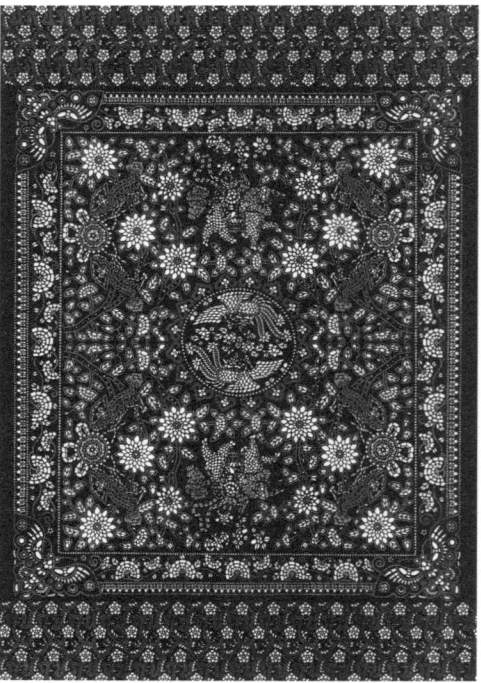

Figure 1.61 The "Phoenix Playing with Peony" quilt top pattern of the Qing Dynasty (from the *Compendium of Chinese Blue Calico Patterns* by Wu Yuanxin)

Figure 1.62 The "Qilin Bringing Sons" quilt top pattern of the Qing Dynasty (from the *Compendium of Chinese Blue Calico Patterns* by Wu Yuanxin)

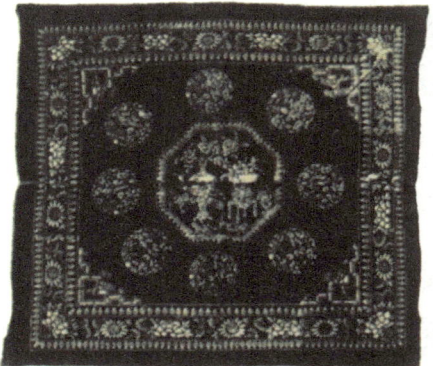

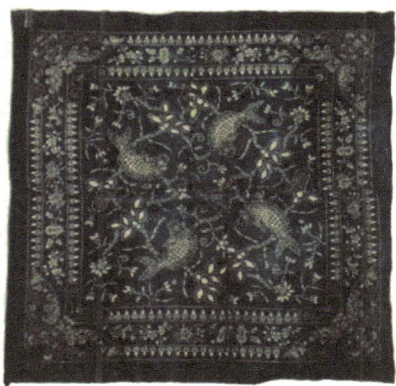

Figure 1.63 The "Wealth and Peace Pattern" wrapping cloth of the Qing Dynasty (from *Splendid China: Blue Calico Cloth of Nantong* authored by Wu Yuanxin and Wu Lingshu)

Figure 1.64 The wrapping cloth with the "Goldfish Playing with Lotus" of the Qing Dynasty (from *Splendid China: Blue Calico Cloth of Nantong* authored by Wu Yuanxin and Wu Lingshu)

The "Wealth and Peace Pattern" wrapping cloth of the Qing Dynasty (Figure 1.63) features chrysanthemums, peonies, and a treasure vase, symbolizing longevity, wealth, and peace, respectively. The design is arranged within a square floral window filled with round chrysanthemums and flowing leaves. At the center of the window, blooming flowers accompany the treasure vase, encircled by eight round peonies. The overall design is distinctive and innovative, vividly conveying the essence of wealth and peace.

Figure 1.64 shows the wrapping cloth with the "Goldfish Playing with Lotus" from the Qing Dynasty. This pattern is often used for wrapping items in dowries. Fish motifs, commonly found in blue calico prints, include popular patterns like "Abundance of Good Fortune" and "Carp Jumping Over the Dragon Gate." In folk reproductive beliefs, fish symbolize strong fertility and numerous offspring, making them frequent in wedding patterns.

Figure 1.65 presents the restored pattern of the wrapping cloth with the "Five Blessings Embracing Longevity" from the Qing Dynasty. This motif, embodying the traditional Chinese aspiration for blessings, refers to longevity, wealth, health, virtue, and a good end. The word for bat, "fu" (蝠), is a homophone for "blessings," hence five bats are used to represent the five blessings. They surround a symbol of longevity, either the character "shou" (寿) or a longevity peach. Known as "Five Blessings Embracing Longevity," this pattern symbolizes a life of prosperity and

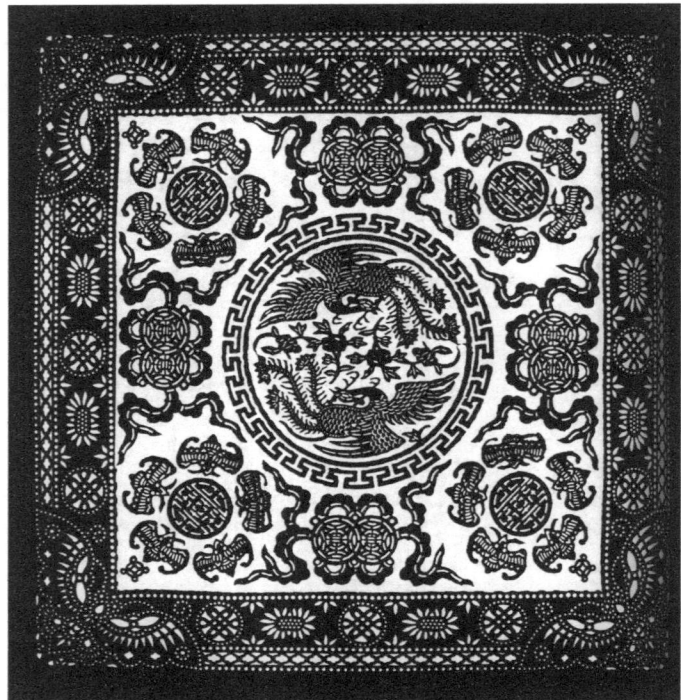

Figure 1.65 The wrapping cloth with the "Five Blessings Embracing Longevity" of the Qing Dynasty (from the *Compendium of Chinese Blue Calico Patterns* by Wu Yuanxin)

extended lifespan. The design of the wrapping cloth is simple yet intricate, with a well-structured pattern and meticulously detailed depictions.

Figure 1.66 showcases a restoration of the "Eight Immortals Crossing the Sea, Three Stars Shining Brightly" curtain pattern from the Qing Dynasty. The curtain is composed of three separate panels depicting immortal figures. The left and right panels feature the "Eight Immortals," widely known in Taoism for their righteousness and benevolence. The famous story "Eight Immortals Crossing the Sea" recounts their journey to celebrate the birthday of the Queen Mother of the West, each displaying their unique powers to cross the ocean. The center panel represents the "Three Stars": the gods of Fortune, Prosperity, and Longevity. Though seemingly incongruous, integrating the "Eight Immortals" and "Three Stars" in one scene symbolizes the belief that life flourishes under their combined auspices. The portrayal of each immortal is vibrant and distinctive, showcasing the mastery of folk artisans in character depiction and carving skills.

Pursuing personal beauty and displaying one's status within social groups are innate human traits. Thus, since the emergence of textiles for warmth and coverage, people have been experimenting with various fabric colors and patterns to express

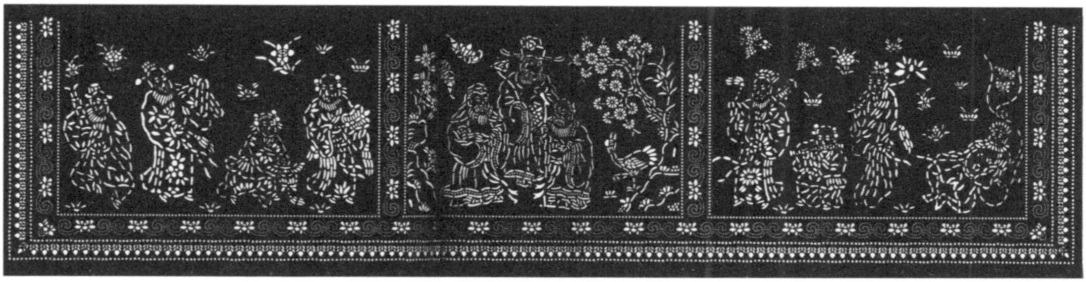

Figure 1.66 The "Eight Immortals Crossing the Sea, Three Stars Shining Brightly" curtain pattern of the Qing Dynasty

their preferences, thoughts, and societal positions. In the palette of antiquity, coloration materials fell into two categories: mineral pigments and plant dyes, with plant dyes being the mainstream. The dyeing techniques developed around the properties of these plant dyes and remained substantially unchanged for a long time. The plethora of color-rich textile artifacts presents us with a remarkable level of sophistication achieved by ancient plant dyeing techniques.

CHAPTER II

Dyeing the Hues of Autumn Mist in Blue-Green— The Art of Dyeing

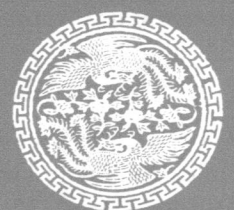

1. The Emergence of Plant Dyes

1.1 The First Coloring Materials Used—Mineral Pigments

Based on existing data, nature provides easily accessible mineral pigments that can be used directly without complex processing, such as hematite and cinnabar. Hematite, also known as ochre, is widely distributed in nature, primarily composed of iron oxide (Fe_2O_3), and exhibits a brownish-red or brownish-orange color. It creates stable and long-lasting but somewhat dull-colored coatings. Cinnabar, also known as vermilion, mainly consists of mercury sulfide (HgS) and is known for its pure, bright, and vivid red hue with good lightfastness. Ancient people used these minerals for coloring ornaments and, driven by the worship of the sun, fire, or blood, also included them as grave goods. Hematite powder and ornaments colored with hematite have been found at the Peking Man site at Zhoukoudian. In the cemetery of Majia cave culture at Liuwan in Qinghai from the late Neolithic period, a male corpse was found sprinkled with cinnabar underneath, suggesting hematite and cinnabar were among the earliest coloring materials used.

1.2 How Plant Dyes Were Discovered

The use of plant materials for dyeing, both archaeologically and from literary sources, seems to have started later than mineral pigments. However, according to legend, it dates back to the time of Emperor Huangdi (Yellow Emperor), around five to six thousand years ago, as many ancient texts mention, "Yellow Emperor making dark caps and yellow skirts, dyeing them with the juices of grass and trees." By then, agricultural production was highly developed, making the emergence of grass dyeing feasible. Considering the use of mineral pigments, it seems plausible that plant dyes were also being used at the time, likely direct dyes from plants that could be applied without complex processing. While this is speculative due to the lack of archaeological evidence, given the abundance and easy availability of dye plants and their superior colorfastness compared to mineral pigments, it's unlikely they went unnoticed and unused.

Plant pigments are hidden in their roots, stems, leaves, or fruits and flowers. How might ancient people have discovered their use as coloring materials? There are several theories.

(1) Direct primitive discovery: Early humans, instinctively attracted to nature's colorful flowers and green leaves, might have picked them and soaked them to extract their juices for dyeing fabrics.

(2) Discovery during food consumption: The legend of Shennong tasting hundreds of herbs to discover edible grains reflects a process of exploration and discovery. During this process, the pigments in some plants may have been noticed.

(3) Discovery during medicine making: According to legend, Shennong also discovered medicinal herbs. During the process of boiling these herbs, colorful and dense solutions were produced, suggesting their potential as dyes.

(4) Discovery through the use of spices: Aromatic plants, such as turmeric, were utilized from ancient times, and they were described as having a "fragrant root and yellow color." During the Zhou Dynasty, turmeric was added to the brewing process, resulting in a wine that was both fragrant and yellow.

2. *The Maturity and Great Development of Plant Dyeing Techniques*

2.1 Colors of the Xia, Shang, and Zhou Dynasties

Although the use of plant dyes dates back to the Neolithic era, it wasn't until the Xia and Shang dynasties that there were written records of large-scale cultivation of some dye plants. The *Xia Xiaozheng* (*The Seasonal Norms in Ancient China*), a book passed down from the Xia Dynasty, not only records the phenology, meteorology, and astronomy of the 12 months of the year but also significant agricultural activities, including the cultivation of indigo plants. By the Zhou Dynasty, plant dyeing had evolved into a more complete set of techniques, becoming the primary dyeing method and an independent craft. This period saw a qualitative leap in the variety and quantity of dye plants, as well as advancements in dyeing techniques. Consequently, specific institutions and officials were established to manage the dyeing process in the Zhou Dynasty. During the Spring and Autumn period, plant dyeing became the mainstream dyeing method, with techniques like direct, overdyeing, and mordant dyeing becoming widespread and skillfully employed (Figures 2.1, 2.2). However, dyeing was greatly affected by seasons due to immature storage techniques for dye plants. Common dye plants included *Indigofera tinctoria*, madder, purple gromwell, *Arthraxon hispidus*, and soap pod. And in relation to color, there are more than ten Chinese characters that are constructed with "纟," such as "红" (red), "紫" (purple), "绛" (crimson), "缁" (dark), and "綦" (dark gray).

The emergence of color-specific characters in the script signifies the high standardization of dyeing operations and the widespread use of color standards for

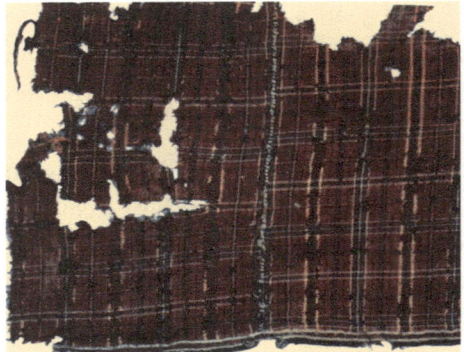

Figure 2.1 Square grid patterned tapestry in the Western Zhou Dynasty

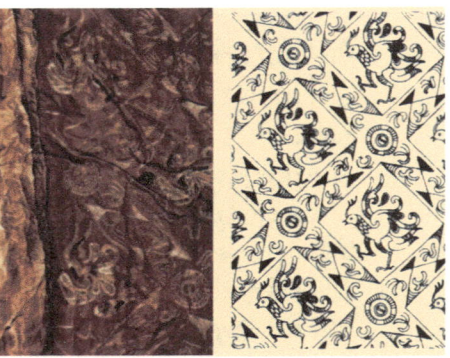

Figure 2.2 Rhombic phoenix bird pattern embroidery of the Warring States period

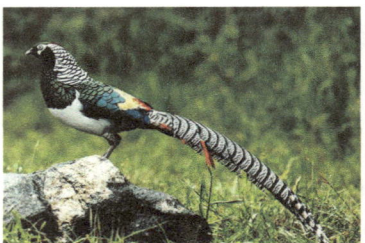
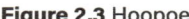

Figure 2.3 Hoopoe

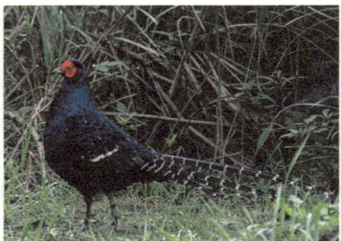

Figure 2.4 Sparrowhawk

comparison. In terms of standardization, *Rites of Zhou · Celestial Officials · Dyers* records, "Dyers are responsible for dyeing silk and hemp. All dyeing should be arranged according to the season, with spring dedicated to bleaching, summer for dyeing the light red color, and autumn for dyeing summer fabrics, while winter is reserved for presenting achievements." This implies a seasonal approach to dyeing, aligning with climatic conditions and fabric quality preservation. Regarding color standardiza-

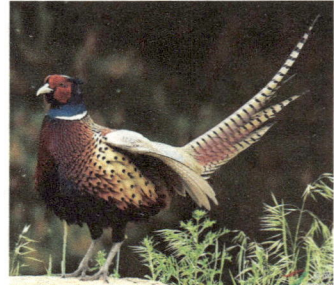

Figure 2.5 Pheasant

tion, feathers of birds like the hoopoe, sparrowhawk, pheasant, and several others were used as color standards. For example, the "hoopoe" might be the golden pheasant (Figure 2.3); the "sparrowhawk" could be the black francolin or the koklass pheasant (Figure 2.4); and the "pheasant" could possibly be the ring-necked pheasant (Figure 2.5).

2.2 Colors of the Qin and Han Dynasties

During the Qin and Han periods, dyeing techniques inherited the traditions of the pre-Qin Dynasty and further developed, especially in terms of the color palette, which expanded rapidly with the increase in dye plant varieties. According to statistics, a vast array of colorful silk, embroidery, linen, and woolen fabrics in over thirty different shades such as vermilion, deep red, bright red, pinkish-red, deep blue, light blue, navy blue, sky blue, dark brown, light brown, dark yellow, light yellow, orange-yellow, golden yellow, leaf green, oil green, emerald green, dark purple, eggplant purple, silver gray, off-white, dark gray, black, and others were unearthed from the Mawangdui Han Tomb in Hunan and the Eastern Han site in Minfeng, Xinjiang. These artifacts vividly showcase the Han Dynasty's dyeing techniques and the dyers' proficiency in immersion, overdyeing, and mordant dyeing skills. Additionally, there was a significant increase in specific terms for various color hues, including close hues of red, orange, yellow, green, cyan, blue, purple, black, and white, reflecting the dynasty's aesthetic sensibilities, human emotions, achievements in dyeing technology, and the endless pursuit of colors (Figures 2.6, 2.7).

The dyers in the Han Dynasty used a variety of tools to achieve these and even more exotic colors, as evidenced by literary records and unearthed artifacts. Volume 4 of *Qin-Han Jinwen Lu* (*Qin and Han Bronze Inscriptions*) includes a full replica of the "Dyeing Furnace of the Ping'an Marquis Family," inscribed with "The tenth dyeing furnace of the household of Marquis Ping'an, weighing six *jin* and three *liang*." Another artifact, the "Bronze Dyeing Cup of the Shi Marquis Family," from Volume 6 of *Taozhai Jijin Lu* (*The Golden Treasury of Tao Zhai*), is inscribed with "The fourth dyeing cup of the household of the Marquis Shi, weighing one *jin* and fourteen *liang*." Experts believe they were used for dyeing, with the furnace

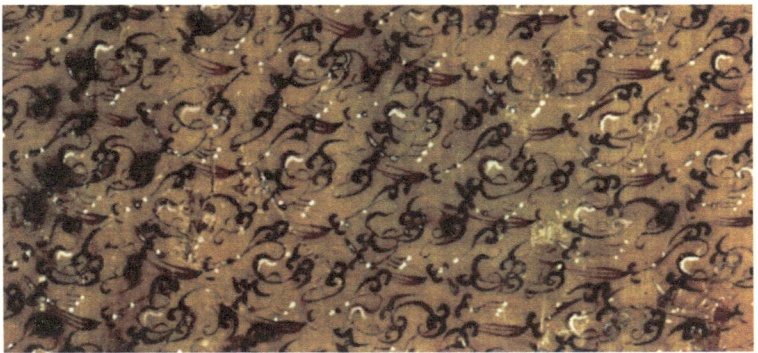

Figure 2.6 Printed and colored gauze of the Western Han

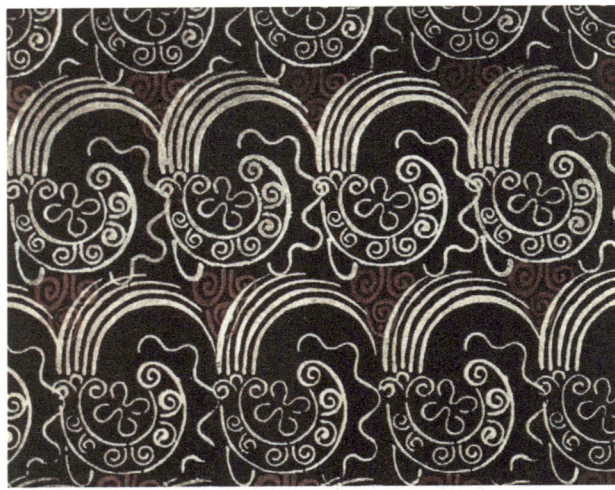

Figure 2.7 Variant swirling cloud pattern colored printed silk of the Western Han (replica)

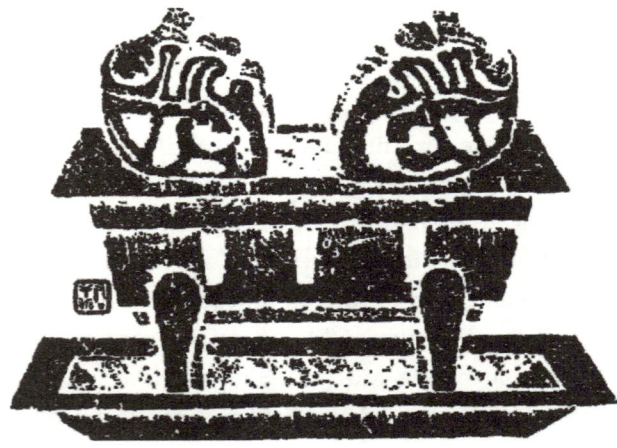

Figure 2.8 Dyeing Furnace of the Ping'an Marquis Family

measuring only 13.2 centimeters in height and 17.6 centimeters in length (Figure 2.8) and the cup weighing about 500 grams, indicating they were not for mass fabric dyeing but rather for trial dyeing or dyeing small bundles of silk or thread for embroidery. A red pottery stove with five figurines and three eyes (Figure 2.9), unearthed in 1954 in Guixian (now Guigang City), Guangxi, from an Eastern Han tomb, is another example. The stove features three vessels—a double-eared pot, and a rice steamer, with two figurines operating beside it. One figure is depicted lifting dyed cloth from the central pot, while the other seems to be adding substances to the pot. The two figurines on each side are scooping water into jars, suggesting the item is a model of a dyeing workshop.

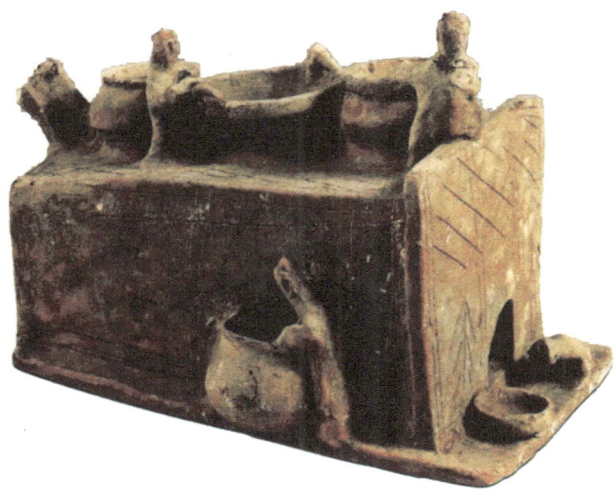

Figure 2.9 Five-figurine three-eyed red pottery stove of the Eastern Han Dynasty

2.3 Colors of the Tang and Song Dynasties

During the Tang and Song dynasties, the variety of plant dyes significantly expanded, and there were substantial advancements in the cultivation, processing, pigment purification, and use of mordants in plant dyeing. Recorded dye plants increased to over thirty types during this period, and a number of color terms appeared in Tang poetry and Song lyrics. For instance, in the *Hua'an Ci Xuan* (*Flower Hermitage Anthology of Poetry*) compiled by Huang Sheng, the color terms are categorized into six groups: reds, purples, yellows, blue-greens, whites, and blacks.

The reds include red, vermilion, crimson, dark red, scarlet, ocher, and cinnabar, with variations like purple-red, faded red, pink, spring red, dew red, fresh red, light red, small red, soft red, dense red, delicate red, green-red, red-white, red-black, high red, cold red, old red, warm red, early red, spotted red, bright red, moist red, red-jade, green-red, red-green, fallen red, congealed red, brilliant red, broken red, lazy red, chaotic red, cheek red, lying red, smudged red, oily red, flying red, purple-vermilion, ocher-yellow, cinnabar, and clouds red.

The purples include purple and navy blue, with variations like emerald purple, golden purple, cyan purple, smoky purple, cloudy purple, greenish-purple, red-purple, purple-red, and navy blue.

The yellows include yellow and gold, with variations like ochre yellow, straw yellow, saffron gold, bee yellow, pale yellow, oriole yellow, goose yellow, willow yellow, deep yellow, and golden yellow.

The blue-greens include blue, green, cyan, slate blue, emerald green, deep indigo, and azure, with varieties like grass green, aquatic green, vibrant fresh green, lush emerald, dense green, willow green, pale light green, vivid green, ethereal misty green, soft tender green, subtle moth green, dewy moist green, verdant grass cyan, mysterious cyan moth, rich teal, verdant mountain green, fresh scallion green, youthful green willow, antique coin green, smoky blue, soft lantern green, precious jade green, deep dark green, traditional vermilion and green, luminous fluorescent green, early spring green, feathered green, smoky grey, expansive vast grey, cliffside grey, ancient grey jade, lichen moss grey, pallid complexion, mossy grey, pure jade, mountain gorge jade, intense deep emerald, petite emerald, lavender-tinted emerald, fading jade, pristine jade disc, contrasting jade and red, cozy warm jade, dark jade indigo, delicate powdered indigo, clear water azure, sky blue azure, meadow grass azure, lightwash azure, crystalline azure, blushed red azure, sunny azure, cyan-tinted azure, gilded azure, and profound deep azure.

The whites include white and pure, with varieties like foamy white, flecked white, cloud-like white, dewy white, sandy white, polished jade white, snowy white, silvery white, daylight bright white, moonlit white, pristine jade, and unblemished white.

The blacks include black, ink, crow, and dark, with variations like night crow, cloud crow, wood crow, and yellow-dark.

The *Flower Hermitage Anthology of Poetry* spans twenty volumes, with the first ten selecting works from Tang and Song scholars, beginning with Li Bai and ending with Wang Mao from the Northern Song, covering 134 poets, and the latter ten volumes featuring works from poets since the mid-Song period, starting with Kang Yuzhi and ending with Hong Fen, covering 88 poets. These color terms in Tang and Song poetry reflect the cultural psychology, aesthetics, and level of color distinction of the period. After all, just like today's pop songs, Tang and Song poetry were not only popular among courts and literati but also among the common folk in streets and markets (Figures 2.10, 2.11).

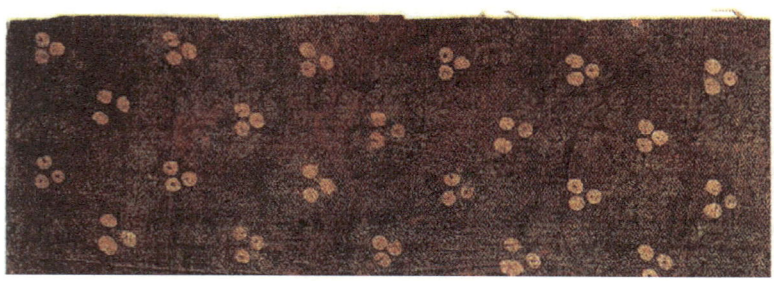

Figure 2.10 Small-dotted flower overlay color printed silk of the Tang Dynasty

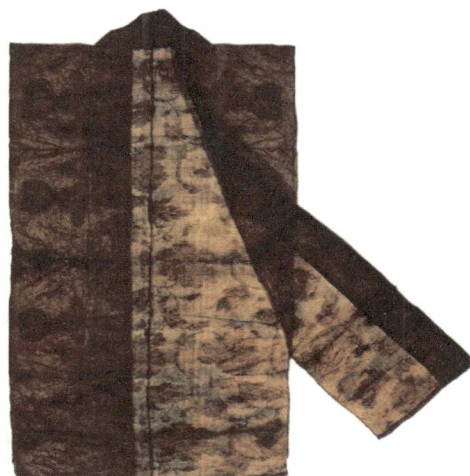

Figure 2.11 Smoky-colored peony flower gauze
vest of the Southern Song Dynasty

2.4 Colors of the Yuan, Ming, and Qing Dynasties

In the Yuan, Ming, and Qing dynasties, plant dyeing technology, whether in terms of the number of dye plant species, the extraction and preservation of dye plants, the use of mordants, or the expansion of the color spectrum, saw significant innovations and progress based on the techniques and experiences of previous eras. The documentation from this period vividly depicts the flourishing state of plant dyeing technology.

In terms of dye plant varieties, Li Shizhen's *Bencao Gangmu* records over fifty kinds of dye plants, with more than thirty explicitly noted for their dyeing properties.

The processing and storage techniques for these plants became increasingly practical. For example, during the Wei and Jin periods, the technique for making safflower cakes was not yet perfected, often leading to mold; hence, the *Qimin Yaoshu* (*Important Methods to Condition the People's Living*) advised against using cakes for "dyeing red." By the Ming Dynasty, the practice of adding Artemisia annua, an antibacterial herb, to the safflower cake mix prevented mold and significantly extended the shelf life of safflower dye. This development led to the use of safflower cakes for "dyeing red" in *Tiangong Kaiwu* (*The Exploitation of the Works of Nature*).

Regarding the use of mordants, the "dyeing methods" recorded in Volume 4 of *Duoneng Bishi* (*Versatile and Practical Affairs*) of the late Yuan and early Ming dynasties include dyeing light red, jujube brown, pepper brown, bright tea brown, dark tea brown, mugwort brown, vitex brown, soap alum method, brick brown, green soap method, white soap method, white Mongolian silk fabric method, iron li fabric method, and soap towel yarn method. Among them, "dyeing light red" encompasses various dyeing techniques, including piece dyeing, over-dyeing, and mordant dyeing. "Dyeing bright tea brown" and "dyeing vitex brown" use a multi-mordant dyeing process with pre-mordanting in alum and post-mordanting in green vitriol. The chapter "Zhang Shi" in the *Tiangong Kaiwu* records thirteen commonly used plant dyes and twenty-seven color dyeing methods, including mordant dyes like sappanwood, black plum, gardenia, sophora, chestnut, and lotus, producing colors like wood red, purple, golden yellow, tea brown, dark red, and various shades of green and cyan.

The expansion of the color spectrum is evident in various texts like *Bencao Gangmu*, *Tiangong Kaiwu*, *Tianshui Bingshan Lu* (*The Collapse of Wealth Under the Sun*), *Cansang Caobian* (*The Tapestry of Sericulture*), *Suzhou Zhizaoju Zhi* (*The Chronicle of Suzhou's Silk Legacy*), and *Yangzhou Huafang Lu* (*Elegance on Water: The Art of Yangzhou's Pleasure Boats*). These sources record a wide range of hues within each color family. For instance, the red family includes shades like red, vermilion, dark red, scarlet, purple-red, ocher-red, iron vermilion, bright red, lotus red, peach red, and so on. The yellow family includes shades like yellow, golden yellow, tender yellow, moth yellow, willow yellow, bright yellow, and more. The green family encompasses jade green, grass green, oil green, bean green, willow green, and others. The blue family has shades like blue, sky blue, emerald blue, treasure blue, and stone blue. The cyan family includes cyan, sky cyan, and original cyan, among others. The purple and brown family features shades like purple, eggplant flower, sauce color, lotus brown, bronze, and brown. The black and white family includes black, crow, soap, dark color, black cyan, white, moon white, ivory white, grass white, onion white, silver color, jade color, reed flower color, and Western white. Volume 1 of *Yangzhou Huafang Lu* mentions that these hues are named in various ways: some after places, like Huai'an Red and Mianyang Green; some by their appearance, such as tender yellow resembling the initial sprout of mulberry, moth yellow resembling the aging of silkworms, and apricot yellow as ancient military attire; some by the name of the dye shop's vat, like grand tutor green referring to the green from the small dyeing vat of the Song Dynasty; and some by customary practice, like mysterious blue, a blend between black and blue, uniting to form a distinct shade. In fact, the color spectrum achieved through dyeing at that time far exceeded this, to the extent that Zhang Jian in *Xuehuan Xiu Pu* (*Shen Shou's Embroidery Manual: A Master's Legacy in the Art of Suzhou Stitching*) mentioned, combining the natural colors of heaven and earth, mountains and rivers, animals, and plants, with variations in depth and intensity, one could achieve a palette of 704 colors. Achieving such a vast array of colors, especially distinguishing dozens of nuanced shades within a single color tone, depended on mastering the combination of dyes, formulas, and process conditions.

Additionally, the *Mumian Pu* by Chu Hua records, "Dye workshops included the blue workshop, dyeing azure, light blue, and moonlit white; the red workshop, dyeing bright red and dew peach red; the bleaching workshop, turning coarse yellow into white; and the mixed colors workshop, dyeing yellow, green, black, purple, bronze, ink, blood tooth (a reddish color), camel fluff, shrimp green, and Buddha face gold, among others." Thus, it's evident that dye workshops were named for the colors they produced, with different hues generally made by separate workshops. At that time, dyeing necessarily involved stoves, and stoves' widespread use to heat dye solutions was a very common technique in dye workshops (Figures 2.12, 2.13, 2.14, 2.15).

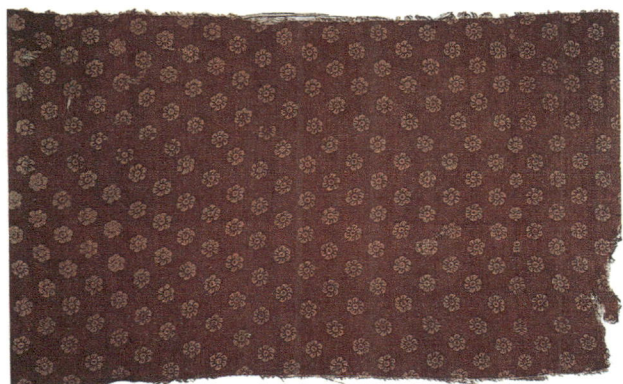

Figure 2.12 Red ground printed silk of the Yuan Dynasty

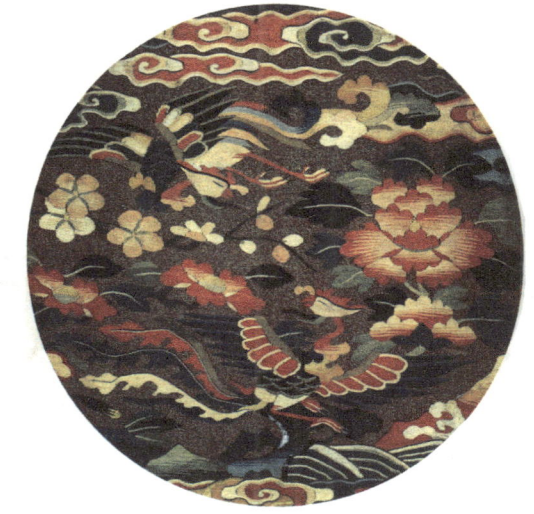

Figure 2.13 Round gold ground phoenix bird pattern kesi patch of the Ming Dynasty

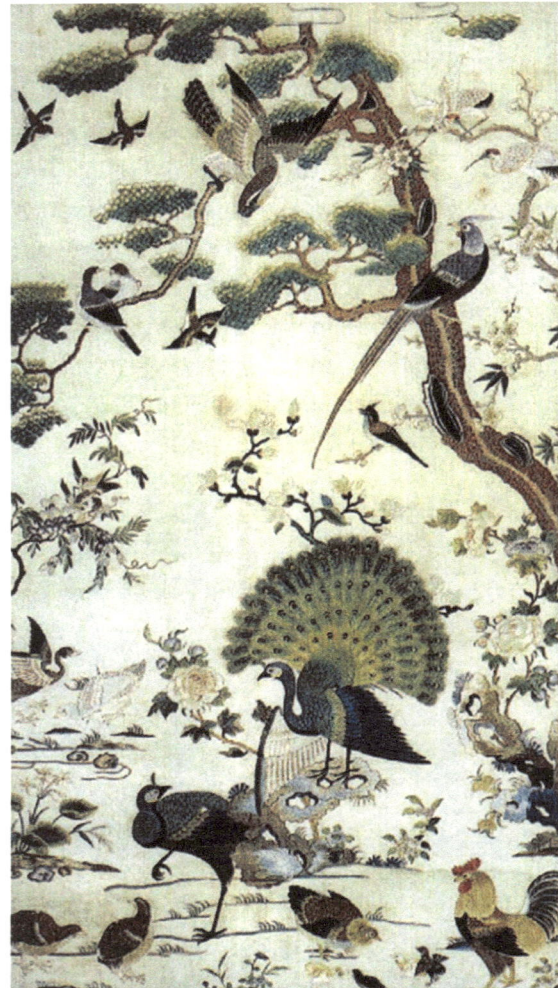

Figure 2.14 Peacock tail spread Guangdong embroidery of the Qing Dynasty

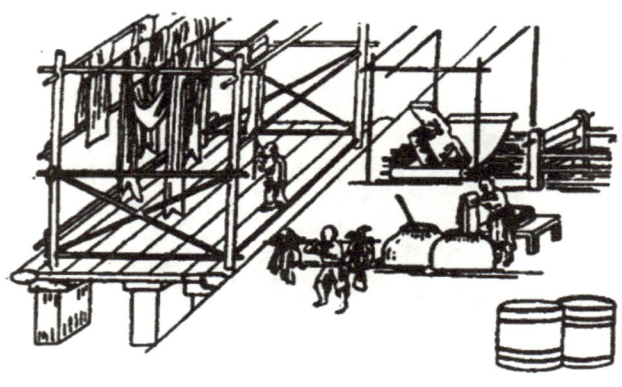

Figure 2.15 Traditional method of dyed cloth of the late Qing Dynasty

3. Types of Plant Dyes

Ancient documents record over fifty types of dye plants. Here, we introduce some significant dye plants, categorized by the primary colors they produce: yellow, red, blue, purple, green, and black.

3.1 Yellow Dye Plants

Among the many dye plants, those yielding yellow hues are the most abundant, with over ten types documented, such as *Arthraxon hispidus*, gardenia, amur cork tree, pagoda tree flower, and *Rehmannia*.

 Arthraxon hispidus (Figure 2.16) is also known in ancient times as lush bamboo, green bamboo, *wang chu*, and *li* grass. It belongs to the Poaceae family and is an annual, delicate herbaceous plant with ovate-lanceolate leaves resembling bamboo, thriving on grassy slopes or in damp areas. The use of this plant for dyeing dates back to early history, with several references found in the *Shijing* (*Book of Songs*). For instance, the *Odes Of Wei · Qi Yu* says, "Behold by riverside, green bamboos in high glee." In the *Odes Of Bin · Qi Yue*, it's mentioned, "In August, we gather rush and reed." In the *Odes Of Bei · Lu Yi*, the lines "My upper robes are green; yellow my lower dress" and "My upper robes are green; yellow my dress with dots" are found. Also, the *Minor Odes of the Kingdom · Cai Lu* states, "I gather all the morn king-grass, but get not a handful, alas!" These references indicate that during the Spring and Autumn period, the technique of using *Arthraxon hispidus* for dyeing yellow or green was already well-developed. Additionally, these texts suggest that the plant was not cultivated at that time, and due to high demand, wild harvesting was common, to the extent that a person's morning collection would not suffice to fill both hands.

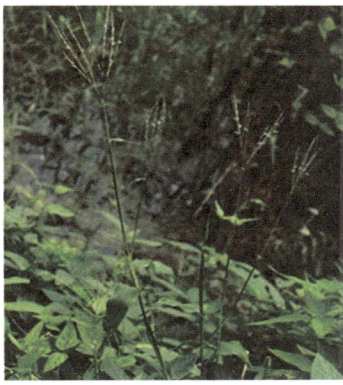
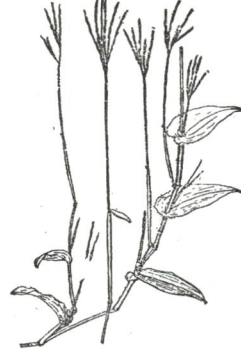

Figure 2.16 *Arthraxon hispidus*

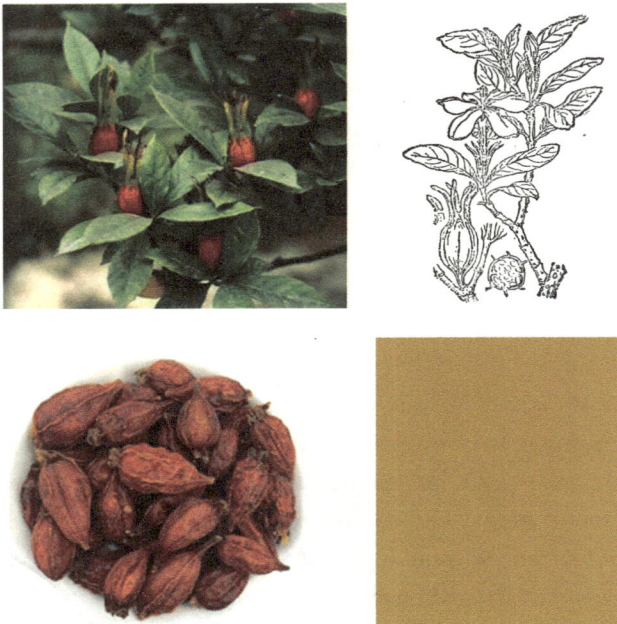

Figure 2.17 Gardenia

Arthraxon hispidus stems and leaves contain a flavonoid compound called arthraxonin. Generally, flavonoids can directly dye fabrics or be used in a dye bath with mordants to color textiles. When directly used, *Arthraxon hispidus* liquid dyes silk and wool fibers a bright yellow. When combined with indigo in a process known as double dyeing, it yields a green color. This usage corresponds with its other name, "green," indicating its historical use combined with *Indigofera tinctoria* to achieve green hues.

Gardenia (Figure 2.17), belonging to the Rubiaceae family, is an evergreen shrub widely found in the southern and southwestern provinces of China. During the Qin and Han dynasties, gardenia was the most extensively used plant for yellow dye. Owing to the insufficient supply of wild gardenia, large-scale cultivation began, as depicted in Sima Qian's *Shiji* (*Records of the Grand Historian*), which states that "thousand mu of gardenia fields could yield profits comparable to that of a marquis." This reflects the scale and profitability of gardenia cultivation in early Han times and its widespread use for yellow dyeing. Various shades of yellow textiles unearthed from the Mawangdui Han Tomb in Changsha were analyzed and found to be dyed with gardenia, either directly or with the addition of mordants.

The fruit of the gardenia contains flavonoids like gardenoside, crocetin, and crocin, with crocetin being the primary pigment for yellow dyeing. The best gardenia for dyeing is harvested after frost, especially those with seven ridges. The extraction of gardenia pigment involves soaking the fruits in cold water for a period before boiling the infusion, which dissolves the pigment in water. The resulting dye can directly produce a yellow color or yield varying shades of yellow when combined with different mordants. Without mordants, the dye produces a tender yellow; with chromium mordants, it yields a greyish or olive yellow; with aluminum mordants, a bright yellow; with copper mordants, a greenish-yellow; and with iron mordants, a dark yellow hue.

The Amur cork tree (Figure 2.18), also known as Huang Bai or *Phellodendron*, belongs to the Rutaceae family. It is a deciduous tree primarily found in Northeast and North China, with some distribution in Henan, northern Anhui, Ningxia, and other regions. The wood contains berberine, an alkaline dye, which can be used for dyeing after boiling. It may be the only alkaline pigment dye used in ancient China.

The Pagoda tree flower, also known as "Huai Mi" (Figure 2.19), from the pagoda tree, a deciduous tree in the Fabaceae family, is also known as the Huai tree, Huai Hua, Bean Huai, White Huai, Fine-Leaf Huai, Jin Yao Cai, Protective Tree, and

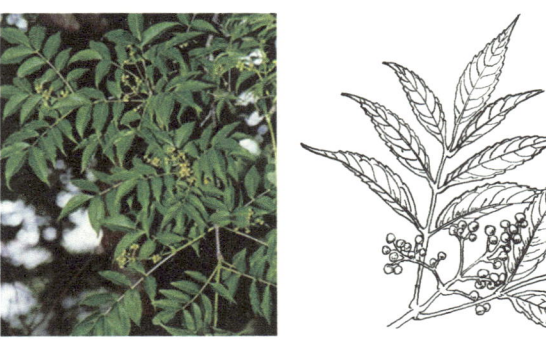

Figure 2.18 Amur cork tree

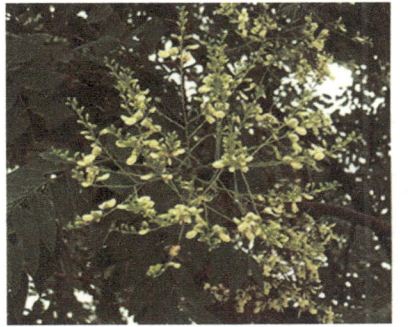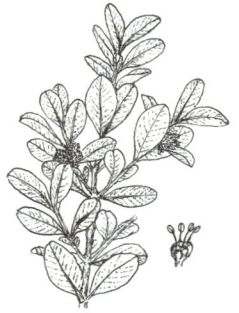

Figure 2.19 Pagoda tree flower

Family Huai. The term "Huai Mi" refers to the flower buds resembling grains of rice. The pagoda tree gained attention as early as the Zhou Dynasty, but records of using its fruit for yellow dyeing only appeared in the Tang Dynasty. From the Song Dynasty onwards, pagoda tree fruit became a mainstream material for yellow dyeing. The dye processing recognized the higher pigment content in the buds compared to the open flowers, leading to the common practice of using both buds and flowers in stages. Pagoda tree cakes were also made for storage, ensuring a year-round supply for dyeing.

The dye components of pagoda tree flowers include yellow sophoricoside and rutin, with a higher concentration in the buds than in the open flowers. This pigment is a mordant dye suitable for dyeing cotton and wool fibers. Using alum as a mordant produces a straw-yellow color, which, when overdyed with indigo, results in an official green; using green vitriol mordant yields a greyish yellow. The flower, known for its bright hue and good fastness, is a relatively new star among yellow plant dyes. The bright yellow color of the imperial robes of the Qing Dynasty was dyed using this pigment.

Rehmannia (Figure 2.20), also known as "Di Huang," belongs to the Scroph-ulariaceae family and is distributed in provinces like Liaoning, Hebei, Henan, Shandong, Shanxi, Shaanxi, Gansu, Inner Mongolia, Jiangsu, and Hubei. Its rhizomes contain rehmannin (or *Rehmannia* glycoside), which can dye fabrics yellow. The *Qimin Yaoshu* detailed the dyeing process of cooked silk with *Rehmannia*, stating, "Pound *Rehmannia* roots until cooked, mix with ash lye, stir evenly, squeeze out the juice, and store in another container. Pound the residue again until thoroughly cooked, mix with ash lye like thin porridge, pour into the vat, and cook raw silk, turning it several times for uniformity. Once the silk is cooked, take it out, put it in a basin, and

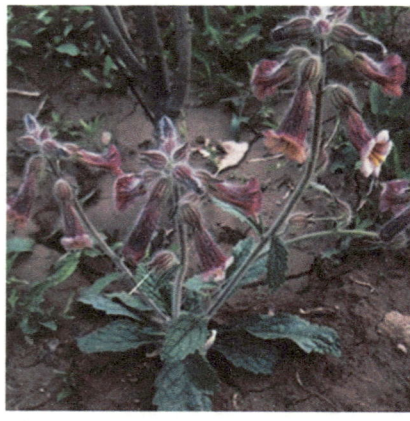
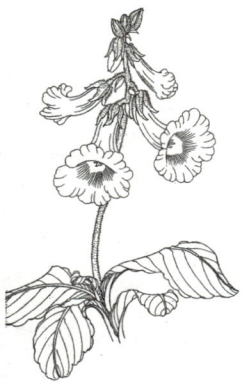

Figure 2.20 *Rehmannia*

stretch it out. After a while, wring out, clean, remove residue, and dry thoroughly. Filter the white juice through another piece of silk, mix it with the hot silk taken out, and dye it in the basin again, spreading quickly for evenness. Once the juice cools, wrings out, and dries, then it's done. Roughly three liters of *Rehmannia* can dye one piece of imperial yellow." This process includes making *Rehmannia* dye, refining silk fabric, and dyeing, with ash lye acting as both a refining agent and a mordant, saving materials and significantly reducing the time for refining and dyeing.

3.2 Red Dye Plants

There are nearly ten types of plants used for red dyes, including madder, safflower, sappan wood, holly, crabapple leaves, and Japanese knotweed. The first three are the most important.

Madder (Figure 2.21) is a perennial climbing herb from the Rubiaceae family. It was the most widely used red dye in ancient times, known by over forty names. Harvested in spring and autumn, the best madder roots are thick and deep red, with autumn harvests superior in quality. Madder-dyed textiles are slightly yellowish-red, vibrant, and beautiful, with good colorfastness, making it a favorite among women in the Spring and Autumn period. References to madder and its dyed clothing are found in the *Book of Songs*. In the 1980s, red woolen textiles were unearthed from a tomb in Zaghunluq, Qiemo (Cherchen) County, Xinjiang, dated around 1000–800 BC. Analysis revealed they were dyed with madder,[1] evidencing the dyeing techniques of the pre-Qin period. From the Western Han Dynasty, madder was extensively

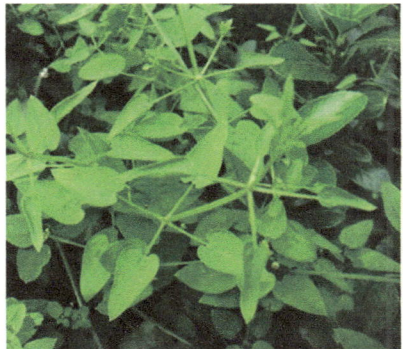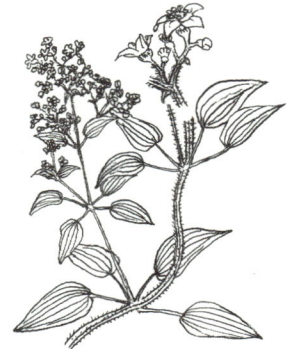

Figure 2.21 Madder

---

1. Xie Yulin, Xiong Yingfei, and Chen Yuansheng, "Identification of the Main Components of Red Dyes on Woolen Fabrics from the Zhou to Han Dynasties," *Conservation and Archaeological Science*, no. 1 (2001): 1–7.

cultivated, with Sima Qian in *Shiji* mentioning significant profits from large-scale madder farming. Mawangdui Han Tomb textiles, like the "Deep Red Silk" and "Longevity Embroidered Robe," were dyed with madder and mordant alum.

Madder roots contain anthraquinone compounds like alizarin, hydroxy alizarin, and pseudohydroxy alizarin. While direct immersion in madder liquid can color fabrics, better results are achieved with metal mordants like aluminum, iron, and copper, yielding a rich array of red shades, especially vivid with aluminum.

Safflower (Figure 2.22), also known historically as "Huang Lan," "Hong Lan," "Red Blue Flower," "Grass Red Flower," "Spiky Red Flower," and "Safflower Grass," is a plant of the Asteraceae family, growing up to 1.5 meters tall. Its leaves are alternately arranged, and it blooms in the summer with red-yellow tubular flowers. Archaeological findings suggest that safflower was among the earliest plant dyes used by humans, dating back to about 5,000 years ago in Egypt. In China, the use of safflower for dyeing came later. It is believed that safflower was first introduced to Northwestern China from Central Asia and then spread to the Central Plains, likely after Zhang Qian's mission to the Western Regions during the Han Dynasty.

The *Taiping Yulan* (*Imperial Readings of the Taiping Dynasty*), citing Xi Zaochi's *Letter to King Yan* from the Eastern Jin Dynasty (AD 317–420), states, "Below here, there are plants with red and blue (safflower); does Your Majesty know of it? People from the north harvest its flowers to dye bright yellow fabrics, and use the part that stops blooming to make 'Yan Zhi' (Yan silk)." This suggests that safflower might have been cultivated and used as a dye in some regions by the Jin Dynasty at the latest. During the Tang and Song periods, safflower was widely cultivated across various regions, including Lingzhou in the Guannei Road, Liangzhou in the Shannan East

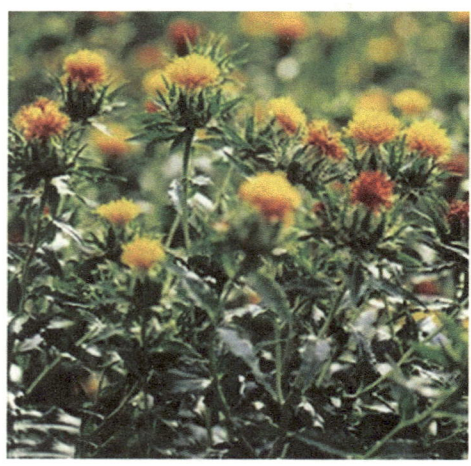
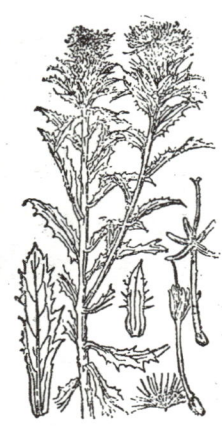

Figure 2.22 Safflower

Road, Quanzhou in the Jiangnan East Road during the Tang Dynasty, and Xinghua Army in Fujian Road during the Song Dynasty, with safflower listed among the tribute products. Furthermore, according to the preface of *Minbu Shu* (*A Detailed Account of Fujian*), from the 15th year of Emperor Wanli's reign (1587), red dyeing with safflower was most famous in Jingkou. At that time in Fujian, since the local red couldn't match the quality of Jingkou's, people from Fujian who traded silk in the lake regions often dyed it emerald red before weaving.

The corolla of the safflower contains two pigments: one is a yellow pigment, making up about 30% of the total; the other is a red pigment, known as carthamin, which constitutes only about 0.5%. Yellow pigment, soluble in water and acidic solutions, had no value as a dye in ancient times. Still, it is commonly used as a safe food coloring additive in modern times. Carthamin, essential for safflower's red dye, is a weakly acidic compound containing phenol groups. It is insoluble in water, dissolving only in alkaline solutions, and precipitates out again when it encounters acid. Although ancient Chinese dyers did not understand the composition and chemical properties of safflower pigments, the methods documented for extracting carthamin are completely consistent with these chemical principles.

Sappanwood (Figure 2.23) is a small evergreen tree of the Legume family, indigenous to Southeast Asia and the Lingnan region of China. However, in ancient times, many believed it to be an exotic plant. Li Shizhen, in his *Bencao Gangmu*, mentioned a "sappanwood country" on an island that produced this wood, hence the name. This misconception likely arose during the Yuan and Ming dynasties when sappanwood was a major import from Southeast Asia to China.

The use of sappanwood for dyeing is first recorded in the Western Jin period by Ji Han in his *Description of Southern Plants*, stating that "The sappanwood tree, resembling the sophora, with black seeds, is found in Jiu Zhen (now Central Vietnam) and is used by the Southern people to dye dark red. Soaking it in the water of the Da Yu region (likely referring to the Meiling mountains on the Jiangxi–Guangdong border) deepens its color."

The reddish-brown heartwood of sappanwood contains a colorless original pigment called "brazilin," which turns into a colored pigment, "brazilein," upon exposure to air. It is soluble in water and can dye wool, cotton, and silk fibers. The resulting colors vary depending on the type of mordant used, ranging from red to purple-black, all exhibiting excellent dyeing fastness. Typically, a chromium mordant yields garnet red to purple, an aluminum mordant results in orange-red, a copper mordant in red-brown, an iron mordant in brown, and a tin mordant in light to deep red. The red color obtained from sappanwood closely resembles that of the safflower

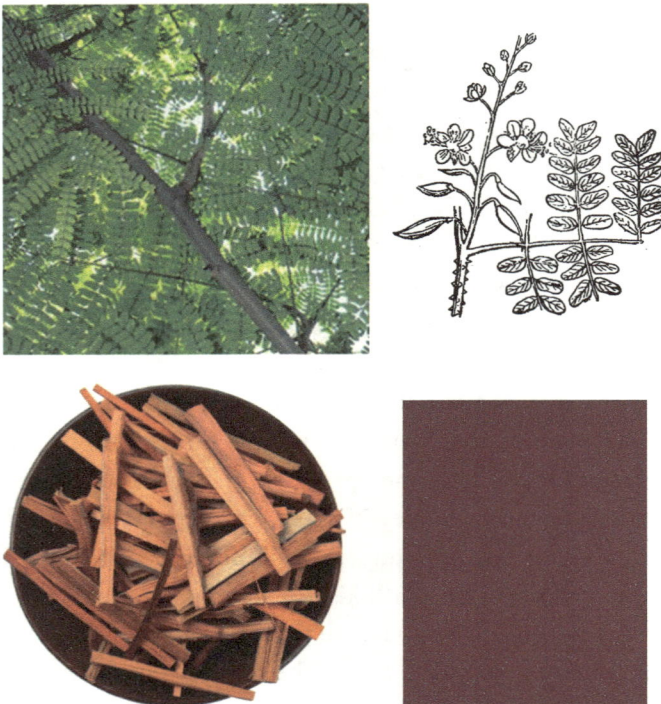

Figure 2.23 Sappanwood

dye used in the Shu brocade and the red color of the Guangxi brocade. Compared to other red plant dyes, sappanwood offers more vivid colors and is easier to extract than safflower.

3.3 Blue Dye Plants

Indigofera tinctoria, the most ancient and widely used blue dye plant, comes in many varieties. Common names for plants used for making indigo include *Persicaria tinctoria, Isatis tinctoria, Isatis indigotica, Polygonum tinctorium, Strobilanthes cusia, Isatis glauca, Isatis indigotica*, and various regional names. Research on these varieties suggests that only four—*Persicaria tinctoria, Isatis indigotica, Strobilanthes cusia*, and *Isatis tinctoria*—were commonly used for dyeing. The variety in names arose from regional differences and the confusion in historical texts, leading to the same species being mistaken for different ones.[2]

---

2. Zhang Haichao and Zhang Xuanmeng, "Research on the Identification of Ancient Chinese Blue-Dye Plants and Related Issues," *Studies in the History of Natural Sciences*, no. 3 (2015): 330–341.

Persicaria tinctoria (Figure 2.24) is known as dyer's knotweed. This annual herb from the Polygonaceae family is typically sown in February or March and harvested in June or July for the first time. A second harvest follows in September or October when new leaves mature. Its cultivation and characteristics have been understood since the Shang and Zhou dynasties. No later than the Shang and Zhou dynasties did people gain a certain understanding of the growth characteristics of the indigo plant. The *Xia Xiaozheng* records, "In the fifth lunar month, when the indigo sprouts, it is necessary to take advantage of the season to separate and transplant the seedlings." The *Xia Xiaozheng Zhuan*, the earliest annotation of this book, explains: "To 'separate' means to thin them out and transplant them. 'Sprout' refers to the gathering of new growth at the right time." Zhang Erqi of the Ming Dynasty further annotates, "The method of planting indigo involves first sowing in seedbeds. When they grow to about five or six inches, they are separated and transplanted. This is what is meant by 'separation.'"

Additionally, the *Liji* (*Book of Rites*) · *Monthly Commands* mentions that in midsummer, "the people are not to cut indigo for dyeing." Kong Yingda's *Zhengyi* commentary elaborates, "At first, indigo plants grow in clusters and will be damaged if transplanted too early. By this month (the fifth lunar month), the indigo has grown large and can now be separated and spread out." Thus, it is evident that people in the pre-Qin period had a deep understanding of the growth characteristics of indigo plants and their extensive usage. The *Liji*'s account aligns with *Xia Xiaozheng*'s record, fully demonstrating this knowledge.

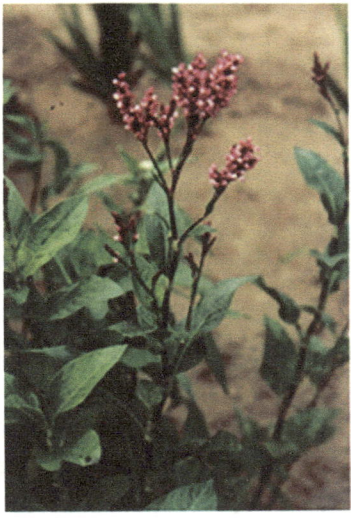 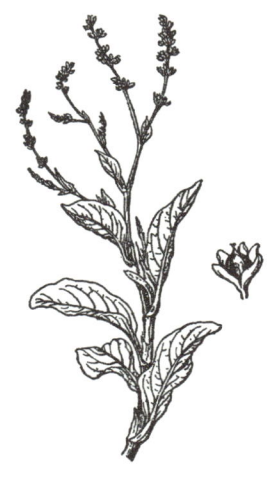

Figure 2.24
Persicaria tinctoria

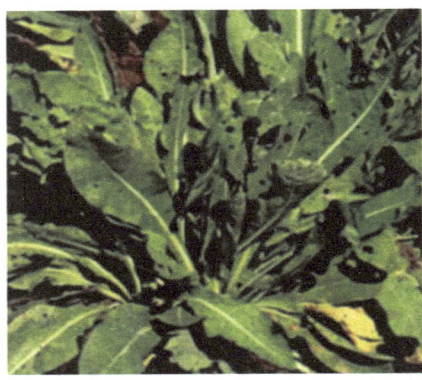
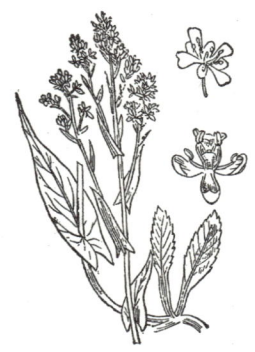

Figure 2.25 *Isatis indigotica*

Isatis indigotica (Figure 2.25) is also known as dyer's woad, glastum, Chinese indigo, or Chinese woad. It is a biennial herbaceous plant belonging to the Brassicaceae family. It features small yellow flowers that bloom atop the plant, with leaves resembling those of spinach or mustard greens. The flowers emerge from the center of the leaves, which are the primary source of the dye. Historical records dating back to the Song Dynasty extensively document its use in producing indigo dye. For instance, Luo Yuan's *Erya Yi* (*Approach to Correct Expressions*) from the Song Dynasty discusses utilizing *Isatis indigotica* to achieve a blue dye. Further mentions include *Zhishun Zhenjiang Zhi* (*The Comprehensive Chronicle of Zhenjiang during the Zhi Shun Era*) of the Yuan Dynasty, which notes the plant's suitability for making indigo. *Jiuhuang Bencao* (*Herbal for Famine Relief*) of the Ming Dynasty, referencing earlier works, states that *Isatis indigotica* can be used for indigo dyeing, attributing its name to the resemblance of its leaves to those of the woad plant.

Isatis tinctoria (Figure 2.26) is a member of the Acanthaceae family. This plant thrives in humid environments, mainly in subtropical regions of East and Southeast Asia. In Taiwan, it is still commonly referred to as Shan Lan. The use of this plant dates back to ancient times, as recorded in *Erya · Shicao*, "Qin means Baphicacanthus cusia," with Guo Pu's annotation, "Now it's the large-leaf winter indigo."

Strobilanthes cusia (Figure 2.27), a perennial bush from the Fabaceae family, is known as Chinese indigo, large indigo, or small woad. It reproduces through seeds and has been used for dyeing since the Han Dynasty. Li Shizhen's *Bencao Gangmu* provides a detailed description of its characteristics.

The principle behind indigo dyeing involves the indigo substance ($C_{14}H_{17}NO_6$) in the leaves. When soaked in water, it ferments and releases soluble indoxyl, turning the liquid yellow-green. Indoxyl further breaks down enzymatically into indigotin, a sugar-derived compound in the plant's cells. Upon exposure to air, indigotin oxidizes

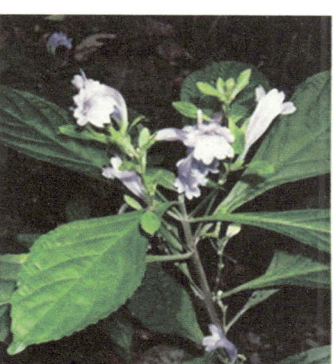
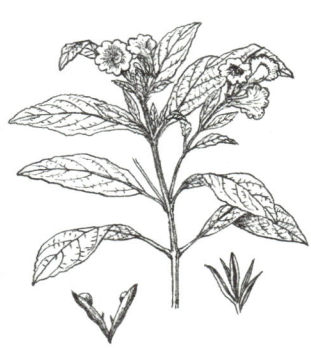

Figure 2.26 *Isatis tinctoria*

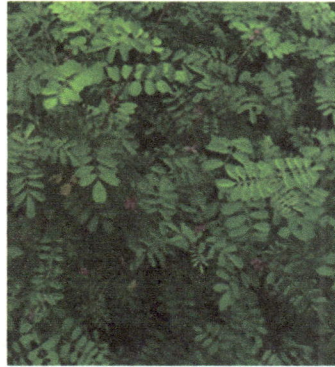
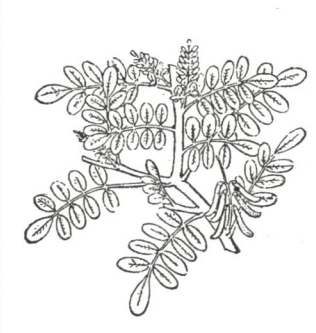

Figure 2.27 *Strobilanthes cusia*

and forms insoluble indigo blue ($C_{16}H_{10}N_2O_3$), which precipitates out. Indigo is a typical vat dye known for its excellent wash and lightfastness.

3.4 Purple Dye Plants

In ancient times, the plants used for dyeing purple include dyer's bugloss, purple sandalwood (also known as "Qinglong Wood"), wild amaranth, and basella, among which dyer's bugloss was the most effective and widely used for producing purple dye across various regions.

Dyer's bugloss (Figure 2.28), historically known as "Zi," "Miao," "Zidan," and "Zijing," is a perennial herb of the Polygonaceae family. Its pigment is primarily located in the roots, typically harvested during August and September when the stems and leaves wither. Dyer's bugloss dyeing flourished in Shandong Province as early as the Spring and Autumn period. The *Guanzi · Qing Zhong Ding* (*Guanzi · Light and Heavy Labor*) records that the people of Lai were skilled in dyeing with drasix

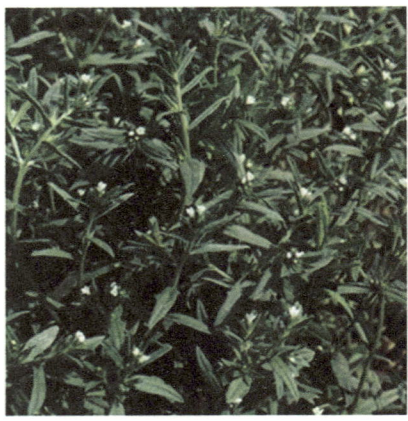 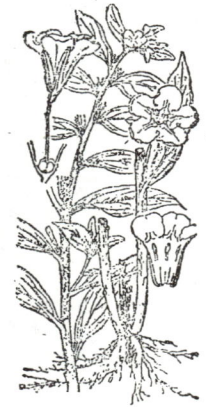

Figure 2.28 Dyer's bugloss

arnebiae, producing a deep black color. "Lai" refers to the eastern part of the ancient Qi state. This passage means that the Qi people were adept at the dyeing process, using dyer's bugloss to dye "pure black" due to the Qi ruler's fondness for purple.

Han Feizi recounts an incident where Duke Huan of Qi's preference for wearing purple led to the entire state adopting purple attire. At the peak of this trend, five pieces of plain clothing could not be traded for one piece of purple garment. When the Qi ruler attempted to curb this practice, it was almost ineffective until Guan Zhong advised him to stop wearing purple himself and to tell his ministers who wore purple to court that he "detested the smell of purple clothes," making them stand back. Following this strategy, the popularity of purple attire was successfully restrained. In *Rites of Zhou*, colors are categorized into primary and secondary colors, with blue, red, yellow, white, and black being the "five primary colors." The colors green, crimson, azure, purple, and sulphur yellow derived from mixing primary colors are considered "secondary colors." Purple, as a secondary color, was contrary to the preferences outlined in *Rites of Zhou*, and was deeply frowned upon by Confucianists. Representative figures like Confucius and Mencius expressed their disdain with statements like "detesting purple for outshining red" and criticizing society's moral decay reflected in the misuse of colors. Furthermore, historical records indicate that during the Tang and Song dynasties, dyer's bugloss of superior quality was produced in regions such as Tangzhou in Shannan Dao, Chengdu and Shu prefectures in Jiannan Dao, Qingzhou in Henan Dao, Jinzhou and Luzhou in Hedong Dao, and Weizhou in Hebei Dao, all of which were presented as a tribute to the court.

Dyer's bugloss is a typical mordant dye. The main chemical components of its pigment are naphthoquinone derivatives, shikonin, and acetylshikonin. Both types of shikonin have poor water solubility, and without a mordant like ash from the

Ailanthus tree or alum, silk, hemp, or wool fibers cannot be dyed. Thus, the use of these mordants is essential for achieving a purple or purplish-red color.

3.5 Green Dye Plants

Historically, green garments were often created through overdyeing or combining dyes, with few plants capable of directly dyeing green. The most renowned among these is *Rhamnus*.

Rhamnus (Figure 2.29), also known as "Frozen Green," "Mountain Plum," and "Zhu Li," is a perennial deciduous small tree or shrub. Because it can directly dye fabrics green, it is also referred to as "Chinese Green." The use of *Rhamnus* for dyeing dates back to ancient times. German author G. Zahn, in his work *A History of Dyeing*, specifically on China, writes, "In ancient times, one of the most famous substances was a green dye, known in Chinese as green fruit (Lao ko). This dye was made from various species of *Rhamnus* shrubs. Both the wood and the juicy fruit of these trees were dyed with a deep yellow pigment. When their concentrated extract is combined with alum and potassium carbonate, it forms a green plant dye. Silk fibers absorb it directly, turning a blue-green color, and it can directly dye plant fibers in a weakly alkaline bath."[3] Zahn believed that the dyeing technique with *Rhamnus* might have appeared around 2000 BC. As referenced in *Taiping Yulan* from Guo Yigong's *Guangzhi* (*The Comprehensive Chronicles*), it is clear that *Rhamnus* was used for dyeing during the Jin Dynasty, though it is not explicitly stated whether it was used to dye green directly.

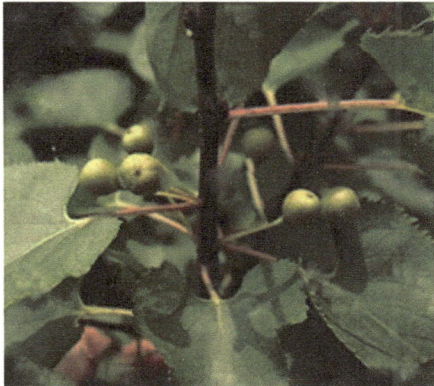 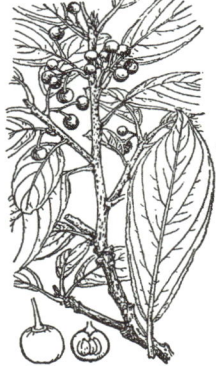

Figure 2.29 *Rhamnus*

---

3. Zhao Feng, "Frozen Green—The Green of China: Study on Ancient Chinese Dye Plants Part Two," *Chinese Agricultural History*, no. 3 (1988): 77–82.

The pigment components of *Rhamnus* include Natural Green 1, Natural Green 2, Rhamnetin, and Methyl Rhamnetin, among others. These pigments contain certain chelating groups, making them suitable for direct fiber dyeing as well as mordant dyeing with metal salts. *Rhamnus* dyes are known for their excellent fastness properties, including resistance to light, acids, and alkalis.

3.6 Black Dye Plants

Various plants have been used for black dyes, including the fruits of *Quercus brantii*, walnuts, bark of the bayberry tree, and lotus seed pods. Among these, *Quercus brantii* has been the most extensively used and is the primary black dye plant of ancient times.

Quercus brantii (Figure 2.30) is a perennial, tall, deciduous tree, also known as oak or tanoak, with its fruit called oak gall. Since black is one of the "five primary colors" and oak gall is a principal black dye, the demand for it has been historically high. The *Rites of Zhou · Officer of Earth* specifically mentions the suitability of mountain and forest flora for producing dye materials. References to oak gall are found in several verses of the *Book of Songs*. The collection and distribution of oak gall were also part of the responsibilities of the "official in charge of dye plants," as recorded in the *Rites of Zhou*.

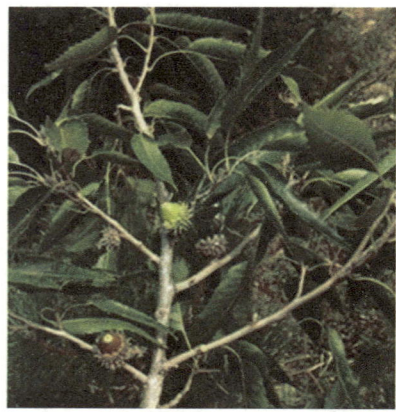 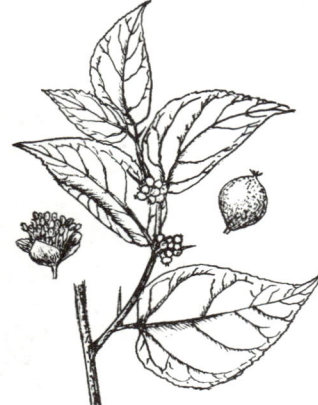

Figure 2.30
Quercus brantii

The fruit and bark of *Quercus brantii* contain various tannins, which are esterified products of gallic acid and hexahydroxydiphenic acid, also known as "complex tannins." Tannin, or tannic acid, is a complex organic compound with multiple phenolic and carboxylic groups, readily oxidizing and polymerizing in the air and easily forming complexes with metal ions. Tannins are water-soluble, allowing for easy extraction by soaking crushed shells and bark in hot water. The ideal water temperature is between 40–50 degrees Celsius; higher temperatures can cause tannins to decompose, while lower temperatures prolong the soaking time. The dyeing mechanism involves adding iron salt mordants to the tannin-extracted dye solution. The tannin initially forms colorless ferric tannate with the iron salts, which then oxidizes in the air to form insoluble ferric tannate. As ferric tannate is a precipitating dye, it firmly adheres to fibers, providing excellent colorfastness.

4. Dye Preparation and Dyeing Process

Ancient dye craftsmen typically categorized dyes into three groups: acid dyes, restoration dyes, and mordant dyes, which also included some direct and alkaline dyes like turmeric, amur cork tree, sumac, oak gall, walnut, and gallnut. Different types of dyes require varied methods of preparation and dyeing techniques.

4.1 Restoration Dye Preparation and Usage—The Case of Indigo

Indigo is a typical vat dye. The initial method of dyeing with indigo involved the fresh indigo leaves fermentation technique, which means directly rubbing indigo leaves together with the fabric, crushing the leaves to let the juice soak into the fabric, or soaking the fabric in a solution fermented from indigo leaves, then taking out the fabric that has adsorbed indican and exposing it to air, allowing the indoxyl to convert into indigo and deposit and fix onto the fibers. This dyeing method was limited by season, as the plant pigments could not be preserved within the plant body for long periods. Freshly picked leaves had to be promptly used for dyeing with the fabric, or else they would lose their dyeing value. Thus, before the development of indigo extraction technology, dyeing could only be conducted during the summer and autumn seasons. The technology for producing indigo appeared around the Wei-Jin period.

Different indigo plants belong to various families, leading to diverse planting and harvesting seasons and varied indigo processing methods. Agronomist Jia Sixie of the Northern Wei described a method using *Isatis indigotica* in his work *Qimin Yaoshu*, "Cutting indigo and placing it upside down in a pit, submerging it in water, and using wood or stones to submerge the leaves fully." The soaking time was "one night in hot weather, another night in cold." The solution was then filtered and placed in a pot, with lime added at a 1.5% ratio, rapidly stirring to accelerate the combination of indoxyl with atmospheric oxygen until the indigo precipitated and the water cleared. Song Yingxing of the Ming Dynasty described in *Tiangong Kaiwu* a method using *Strobilanthes cusia*: soaking leaves and stems in pits, barrels, or vats for seven days, then adding lime to the strained juice. For each batch of slurry, add five liters of lime and stir vigorously dozens of times; the indigo will then coagulate. After the water stilled, indigo settled at the bottom.

The method employed by modern Dong people for extracting indigo closely resembles the techniques described by Jia Sixie, albeit with different tools. Their toolkit for indigo fermentation includes a large wooden barrel, a bamboo sieve crafted from bamboo strips to be slightly smaller than the mouth of the barrel, two wooden sticks, two large stones, a small cloth bag filled with lime, and a basin. The process unfolds as follows: Initially, the indigo plants are cleansed and placed into the wooden barrel, with clean water added to submerge the plants. The bamboo sieve is then positioned on top, secured at the barrel's mouth with the wooden sticks arranged in a cross formation, and the setup is left to soak, covered. The duration of this soaking phase is contingent upon the weather, typically requiring a full day and night under sunny conditions and a longer period when it's cool. By the next day, the water transforms into a blue-green hue, topped with a thin layer of copper-colored substances and white foam, signaling the thorough soaking of the indigo plants. After removing the sticks, sieve, soaked plants, and residuals, lime is introduced in one of two ways: shaking and squeezing lime from a cloth bag submerged in the water or directly shaking lime poured into the barrel to ensure thorough mixing. Following lime addition, the water's color shifts gradually from blue-green to gray-green, and the foam changes from white to blue. The appearance of purple foam signifies an adequate quantity of lime, marking the commencement of "stirring the indigo." This involves stirring the barrel's contents with a large ladle or basin until the foam deepens to a dark blue. This seemingly straightforward step requires expertise, as seasoned indigo beaters can judge the process's completion by observing the "water gate"—the changing color of the indigo water. In contrast, those less experienced may have to taste the water to determine its readiness. Once stirred, the mixture is left covered for 8–12 hours, allowing the indigo to settle at the barrel's bottom. The quality of indigo is assessed by taking a small amount on the hand and examining its color in sunlight: a grayish tint indicates an excess of lime, a dark color suggests overly long soaking, and a deep blue with a reflective quality denotes high-quality indigo (Figure 2.31).

For chemically processed indigo dyeing, indigo is first placed in an acidic solution and mixed with an appropriate amount of brewer's grains. After a period of fermentation, it becomes ready for use as a dye solution. The fabric to be dyed is then soaked in the solution and, upon exposure to sunlight post-removal, turns blue. The dyeing mechanism involves the restoration of indigo to leuco-indigo by hydrogen (and carbon dioxide) produced during the fermentation of brewer's grains. Leuco-indigo is soluble in acidic solutions, allowing the fibers to absorb color. Once dyed and exposed to air, the fabric oxidizes

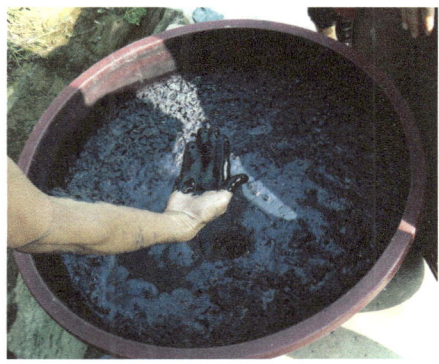

Figure 2.31 Observing the quality of indigo

and exhibits a vivid blue hue. Repeated dyeing is often used in traditional indigo dyeing to increase the uptake rate. This involves repeatedly soaking the fiber or fabric in the same dye solution to gradually deepen the color. Due to the limited affinity between plant dyes and fibers, only a small amount of dye adheres to the fibers in each soak, requiring multiple immersions for a rich color. Moreover, the fabric should not be wrung out but air-dried between successive dyeing sessions to allow more dye absorption in subsequent immersions.

4.2 Acid Dye Preparation and Usage—The Case of Safflower

Safflower, structurally different from modern-defined acid dyes, is considered an acid dye since it only dyes in an acidic bath. As mentioned earlier, safflower contains both yellow and red pigments, but only the red pigment is valuable for dyeing. Modern dyeing science extracts safflower's red pigment by exploiting the properties of both pigments, which are soluble in alkaline solutions, while the red pigment is insoluble in acidic solutions. This involves soaking safflower in an alkaline solution and then adding acid to precipitate only the fluorescent red pigment. This characteristic of safflower has been utilized for purification and red dyeing since the Han Dynasty.

There are generally two forms of prepared safflower dye: dry safflower and safflower cake. The method for making dry safflower is detailed in *Qimin Yaoshu*, involving mashing safflower, fermenting it slightly, rinsing it with water, twisting out the yellow juice with a cloth bag, soaking it in wood ash (an alkaline solution), then in fermented millet porridge (acidic), and finally twisting in a cloth bag for dyeing. The method for safflower cake, first recorded in the Jin Dynasty by Zhang Hua in *Bowu Zhi* (*Records of Natural History*), is described in detail in Song Yingxing's *Tiangong Kaiwu* from the Ming Dynasty, "Pick the safflowers with dew on them, pound them until they are crushed, then wash with water and use a cloth bag to wring out the yellow juice. Pound them again and wash them with the clear liquid from sour millet or rice water. Wash again and use the cloth bag to squeeze out the juice. Cover with wormwood overnight, then knead into thin cakes and dry in the shade before storing. For dyers who have mastered this technique, I, Zhu Kongyang, can produce what is known as scarlet." Adding wormwood in the cake-making process can prevent the safflower cake from molding. To enhance the color, acidic plum water is used instead of fermented millet porridge to precipitate the red pigment. Notably, ancient China not only utilized safflower for dyeing but also managed to re-extract the red pigment from dyed fabrics for reuse. This is clearly recorded in *Tiangong Kaiwu*, "For fabrics dyed with safflower, if one wishes to revert the color, simply moisten the dyed fabric, apply several drops of alkaline water or rice ash water, and the red will be recovered, still in its original form. Store the collected water in mung bean powder, then use it to dye red without any wastage." This seemingly complex method is logical: it uses the property of safflower's red pigment being soluble in alkaline solutions to re-extract it from the dyed fabric. Storing it in mung bean powder utilizes the powder as an absorbent for the red pigment. This technique was mastered as early as the Tang Dynasty, evidenced by many printed fabrics excavated in Turfan, dyed using this principle, suggesting that the special properties of safflower pigment likely led to the development of resist dyeing and printing (Figure 2.32).

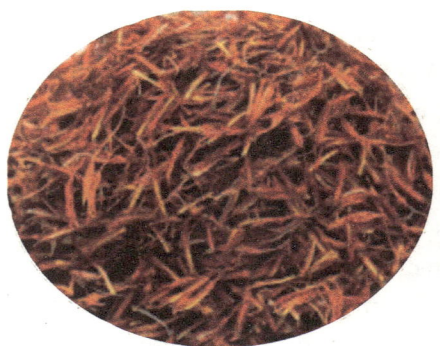

Figure 2.32 The red color dyed with safflower

Safflower dyeing often employs the direct repeat dyeing method. This process involves directly placing the fabric to be dyed into a fermented dye solution containing the plant's branches, leaves, or other pigment-rich parts. Dyeing is achieved through soaking or boiling, depending on the desired shade's intensity, with the fabric immersed or boiled in the same dye solution multiple times. In *Tiangong Kaiwu*, Song Yingxing lists various shades obtained by this method, including bright red, lotus red, peach red, silver red, water red, cyan blue, sky blue, moon white, grass white, ivory color, and wool green cloth color. The method for bright red involves using safflower cake and plum water, then clarifying with alkaline water or substituting rice straw ash, achieving a vivid color after several clarifications. The bright red, lotus red, peach red, silver red, and water red shades use the same technique, with the intensity adjusted according to the amount of safflower cake used.

4.3 Mordant Dye Preparation and Usage—The Case of Purple Gromwell and Pagoda Tree Flower

Aside from a few exceptions, most natural dyes do not inherently possess a strong affinity for fibers and hence cannot directly dye them. Instead, they require metal salt mordants to chemically react with the dye molecule's coordinating groups, allowing the pigments to attach to the fibers as complexes. Mordant dyeing not only works for various fibers, but using different mordants, the same dye can produce a range of colors.

The key to preparing most mordant plant dyes, which are generally extractable directly with water, lies in preserving the pigments. This process is much simpler compared to the preparation of indigo and safflower. Taking purple gromwell as an example, to prevent pigment deterioration during harvest, *Qimin Yaoshu* advises, "Bundle in groups of four, cut evenly on the same day, arrange in long rows upside down, and place on a solid flat surface, weighing them down with plank stones to flatten (moist weight makes it stretch, dry weight causes breakage, without weight it's hard to sell). After two to three days, stand them in the sun to dry (not drying causes blackening, too dry causes breakage)." This not only preserves the pigment well but also makes the product aesthetically pleasing for sale. For pagoda tree flowers, *Tiangong Kaiwu* describes the preparation of pagoda flower cakes, "Unopened flowers, called flower buds, are collected by spreading a dense net below the tree. Boil in water, strain, and squeeze into cakes for dyeing. After drying, mix with a little lime and store." The lime is evidently used for drying to prevent pigment loss, while cake formation aids in transportation and sale.

Without mordants, purple gromwell hardly dyes fibers, and pagoda tree flowers can only dye yellow with poor fastness. Only after adding aluminum or iron salt mordants can they produce orange-yellow, purple, and black colors, respectively, with improved colorfastness, making mordants an essential part of the process (Figures 3.33 and 3.34).

Historically, most mordants were either iron or aluminum compounds.

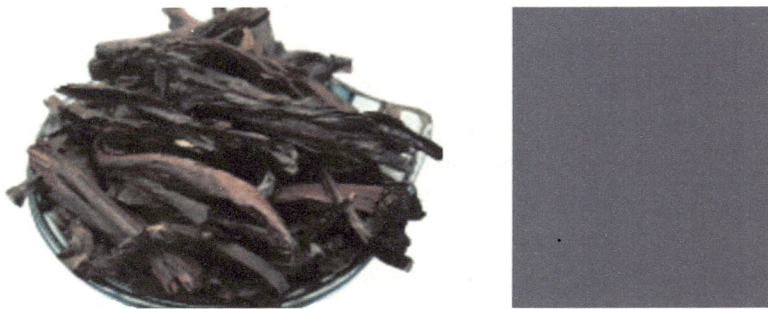

Figure 3.33 The purple color dyed with gromwell root

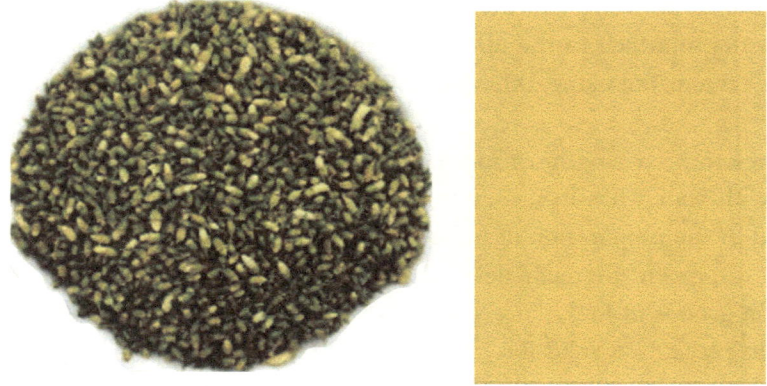

Figure 3.34 The yellow color dyed with pagoda tree flower

The primary sources of iron ion mordants can be essentially narrowed down to three: the slurry from pyrite mines, the green vitriol produced by roasting pyrite, and the iron-containing river mud. Among these, the green vitriol is the most important due to its use in dyeing black; hence, it is also called copperas. Its chemical composition is $FeSO_4 \cdot 7H_2O$, which is soluble in water and can gradually oxidize into iron sulfate in air. The iron ions can be complex with the coordinating groups in the mordant dyes. Among the various alum applications in ancient China, the production technique of this alum was the earliest to appear, and its emergence is very likely related to dyeing with soaps, to the extent that some scholars believe that "the green vitriol produced at that time was mainly used for mordant dyeing in black." Chen Cangqi of the Tang Dynasty recorded a simple method for making iron mordants from rusted ironware in *Bencao Shiyi* (*Supplement to the Materia Medica*), stating, "Take some iron and soak it in water in a vessel; after a long time, when green foam appears, it is suitable for dyeing soaps." The principle is to oxidize the iron in water to form iron oxide, which then converts to iron hydroxide and precipitates, with a very small amount of iron ions acting as a mordant.

Aluminum ion mordants primarily derive from alum, also known as white alum. It is a double sulfate of potassium and aluminum that hydrolyzes upon contact with water, forming a gelatinous aluminum hydroxide substance. The aluminum ions can be complex with coordinating groups in mordant dyes. Alum does not occur naturally and is a product of artificially roasting alumstone. The earliest documented production of alum in China can be traced back at least to the Han Dynasty, as clearly mentioned in the *Taiqing Jinye Shendan Jing* (*The Scripture of the Golden Elixir of Supreme Clarity*), a text believed to be compiled in the later Western Han Dynasty, which specifies the use of alum in its formulas. A minor source comes from the ash of plants containing aluminum ions, with plants historically used for ash production as mordants, including goosefoot, Eurya japonica, sweetgum, and wormwood. According to modern scientific methods, these have all been found to contain rich aluminum elements.

There are four main mordanting techniques: simultaneous mordanting, pre-mordanting, post-mordanting, and multiple mordanting. In simultaneous mordanting, the fabric is dyed directly in a dye bath containing the mordant, as seen in *Qimin Yaoshu* for dyeing imperial yellow with *Rehmannia glutinosa* and dyeing blue with wood ash in indigo dye. Pre-mordanting involves soaking the fabric in a mordant solution before dyeing. Purple gromwell dyeing is representative of this method, as its main pigment components, naphthoquinone derivatives like shikonin and acetylshikonin, have hydrophobic side chains, and pre-mordanting achieves better dyeing results. Post-mordanting is the opposite process of pre-mordanting, where the fabric is first dyed in the dye bath and then soaked in a solution containing the mordant. This method initially uses dyes with weaker affinity to the fiber, allowing the dye to reach equilibrium and even distribution in the dye bath before the mordant helps form a complex on the fabric surface. One of the advantages of post-mordanting over same-mordanting or pre-mordanting is achieving more uniform dyeing and precise color endpoints. A typical example of post-mordanting is dyeing fabric with pagoda tree flowers to achieve an oil-green color. First, the fabric is lightly dyed with pagoda tree flowers and then soaked in a green vitriol solution. The multiple mordanting process involves initially using alum for pre-mordanting, followed by dyeing, and then using green vitriol for post-mordanting. This method starts by binding the fiber with a mordant that forms lighter colors, such as aluminum, through ionic bonds. The pre-mordanted fiber is then dyed, allowing the dye to easily bind and form complexes with existing metal ions. Finally, a deeper-color-forming mordant, like iron, is used to further combine with most of the dye absorbed on the fabric surface or replace the existing aluminum ions, resulting in deeper, more uniform, and durable colors. A representative example is dyeing fabric with sappanwood to achieve a date-brown color, where the fabric is first pre-mordanted with alum, then dyed in sappanwood solution, and finally post-mordanted with green vitriol.

Each dyeing technique varies in effectiveness depending on the specific dye plant used. However, for most mordant dyes, pre-mordanting results in less durable colors and less precise endpoints; simultaneous mordanting challenges even dyeing; post-mordanting is slower, while multiple mordanting generally provides a more rational dyeing process. In summary, mordant dyes generally offer better dye uptake, lightfastness, acid and alkali resistance, and colorfastness compared to other dyes. However, their dyeing process is more complex. If the mordant is not used correctly, the resulting color can significantly deviate from the intended standard and be difficult to correct. Therefore, precise control is crucial to achieve the desired outcome.

Bibliography

Du, Yansun. *Methods of Dyeing with Domestic Plant Dyes*. Shanghai: The Commercial Press, 1970.

Jia, Sixie. *Qimin Yaoshu with Annotations and Explanations*. Annotated by Miao Qiyu. Beijing: Agriculture Publishing House, 1982.

Li, Shizhen. *Bencao Gangmu (Compendium of Materia Medica)*. Beijing: China Medical Science and Technology Press, 2011.

Museum of Xinjiang Uygur Autonomous Region and Unearthed Cultural Relics Exhibition Working Team. *The Silk Road: Han and Tang Fabric*. Beijing: Cultural Relics Publishing House, 1973.

Museum of Xinjiang Uygur Autonomous Region. *Cultural Relics Unearthed in Xinjiang*. Beijing: Cultural Relics Publishing House, 1975.

Native Produce and Animal By-Products Bureau, the Ministry of Commerce of the People's Republic of China and Institute of Botany, Chinese Academy of Sciences. *Flora of Economic Plants of China*. Beijing: Science Press, 1961.

Shanghai Silk Industry Group and Shanghai Textile Research Institute. *Research on Textiles Unearthed from the Han Tomb No. 1 at Mawangdui, Changsha*. Beijing: Cultural Relics Publishing House, 1982.

Song, Yingxing. *Tiangong Kaiwu (Heyday of Agriculture and Handicraft Industry in Ancient China)*. Annotated by Zhong Guangyan. Guangzhou: Guangdong People's Publishing House, 1976.

Wu, Shan. *Encyclopedia of Chinese Arts and Crafts*. Nanjing: Jiangsu Fine Arts Publishing House, 1988.

Wu, Yuanxin, and Wu Lingshu. *Splendid China: Blue Calico Cloth of Nantong*. Suzhou: Suzhou University Press, 2011.

——. *The Soul of Printing and Paste-Resist Dyeing*. Harbin: Heilongjiang People's Publishing House, 2011.

Wu, Yuanxin, Wu Lingshu, and Peng Ying. *Traditional Chinese Folk Dyeing Techniques*. Beijing: China Textile Press, 2011.

Zhang, Qin. *Chinese Blue Clamp Resist Dyeing*. Beijing: Xueyuan Publishing House, 2006.

Zhao, Chengze. *History of Science and Technology in China: Textile*. Beijing: Science Press, 2002.

Zhao, Feng, and Wang Le. *Dunhuang Silk*. Lanzhou: Gansu Education Publishing House, 2013.

Zhao, Hansheng, Xing Shengyuan, and Tian Fang. *Popular History of Textile Technology*. Jinan: Shandong Science and Technology Press, 2015.

Zhao, Kuanghua, and Zhou Jiahua. *History of Science and Technology in China: Chemistry*. Beijing: Science Press, 1998.

Zheng, Juxin. *Chinese Splendor: Southern Zhejiang Clamp Resist Dyeing*. Suzhou: Suzhou University Press, 2009.

Zhu, Xinyu. *A General History of Chinese Silk*. Beijing: Textile Industry Press, 1992.

HUA JUEMING, a researcher and former associate director of the Institute for the History of Natural Sciences at the Chinese Academy of Sciences, is a renowned expert in the history of science and technology in China. His main research areas include ancient bronze metallurgy, steel technology, the history of machinery, and the philosophy of technology. In recent years, he has been devoted to the research and preservation of traditional crafts. He is the author of several works, including *Essays on the History of Chinese Metallurgy, Ancient Chinese Metal Technology, Five Thousand Years of Chinese Science and Technology*, and *Ancient Chinese Metal Technology*.

FENG LISHENG, a researcher and director of the Institute for the History of Science and Ancient Documents at Tsinghua University, is mainly engaged in research on the history of mathematics in China and abroad, the history of Chinese machinery, the history of metrology, the history of physics, and the history of science and technology among Chinese ethnic minorities. He is the author of works such as *The History of Ancient Chinese Surveying* and *The History of Sino-Japanese Mathematical Relations*.

ABOUT THE AUTHOR

ZHAO HANSHENG, Deputy Researcher at the Institute for the History of Natural Sciences of the Chinese Academy of Sciences, specializes in the history of textile technology in ancient China. He has authored contributions in eminent publications, including the textile section in *The Essence of Chinese Literature through the Ages*, the embroidery section in *Illustrated Achievements of Ancient Chinese Science and Technology*, and the materials and spinning sections in the monograph *The History of Science and Technology in China: Textiles*.

ABOUT THE TRANSLATORS

CHEN WEI: PhD, English professor of Jiangnan University, Wuxi, Jiangsu Province, PRC.

XU XIANWEI: MA candidate of Jiangnan University, Wuxi, Jiangsu Province, PRC.